INSIDE THE
ADOPTION AGENCY

OTHER WORKS BY
THE AUTHOR

The Intercountry Adoption Journey: Hague-Compliant Training from the National Council of Adoption, www.hagueadoption.org

Special Needs Children, Exceptional Parents: Their Personal Stories, Los Niños International Adoption Center

How to Adopt Internationally, Mesa House Publishing

Butterflies in the Wind: The Truth about Latin American Adoptions, iUniverse Press

The Reluctant Warrior: Former POW Finds Peace in Texas, Eakin Press

Gamines: How to Adopt from Latin America, Dillon Press

For the history, bio, photos, and videos of Erichsen's work, visit http://erichsenbooks.com

INSIDE THE ADOPTION AGENCY

✦

Understanding Intercountry Adoption in
the Era of the Hague Convention

Jean Nelson Erichsen, MA, LBSW
Cofounder and Codirector of Los
Niños International Adoption Center

iUniverse, Inc.
New York Lincoln Shanghai

INSIDE THE ADOPTION AGENCY
Understanding Intercountry Adoption in the Era of the Hague Convention

iUniverse books may be ordered through booksellers or by contacting:

iUniverse
2021 Pine Lake Road, Suite 100
Lincoln, NE 68512
www.iuniverse.com
1-800-Authors (1-800-288-4677)

Editorial correspondence and requests for permission to reprint should be mailed to Erichsen Consultations, 55 North Country Gate Circle, The Woodlands, TX 77384.

E-mail should be addressed to Jean.Erichsen@gmail.com.

Except in cases where adoptive parents granted permission for their stories to be told, names and places have been changed to ensure privacy.

ISBN-13: 978-0-595-40206-9 (pbk)
ISBN-13: 978-0-595-84582-8 (ebk)
ISBN-10: 0-595-40206-2 (pbk)
ISBN-10: 0-595-84582-7 (ebk)

Printed in the United States of America

ACKNOWLEDGMENTS

I'm exceedingly grateful to my husband, Heino R. Erichsen, for his advice and research based on his incredible knowledge of geography, history, politics, and the Hague Convention. I wouldn't have attempted this without his input.

Other experts in various fields of adoption have made valuable contributions. Deborah McCurdy, founder and adoption supervisor of Beacon House Adoption Agency and proofreader extraordinaire, improved the entire manuscript, added numerous important passages, and suggested the subtitle.

Laura Kalish, attorney; Sandra Carlson, LCSW (licensed certified social worker); and Ruth Arnold, adoptive parent and former Los Niños International Adoption Center (LNI) board member provided valuable input. Rebekah Waye, assistant director of international adoption programs at LNI, added some beneficial paragraphs.

I offer a special thank-you to the staff at Los Niños International Adoption Center, Rebekah Waye, Jason Heck, and Libby Bennett.

Contents

INTRODUCTION

✦

Look before You Leap
(And If You've Already Leaped, Here's How
to Get a Handle on the Situation)

Prospective adoptive parents have an insatiable craving for information, but they must learn to discriminate between the valid and the invalid. Finding out how ethical international adoptions work is paramount before taking that first big step: applying to an adoption agency. Knowing how to compare agencies is another. Yet this book is not a substitute for trusting one's instincts and common sense.

Tips and anecdotes are sprinkled through the chapters to illustrate key issues. In this book, I explain the mysteries of an adoption agency by mapping out the ten parts of the adoption maze.

- Adoption agency founding and funding
- How adoption agencies compete for your application
- Contracts and agreements
- Fees and waiting times
- What the children are like
- Difficulties for adoption agencies securing government agreements and hiring staff abroad
- The hosting of foreign adoption delegations
- Issues of refugee children
- A typical day inside an agency
- The impact of the Hague Convention on future international adoptions

If you want to understand the mysteries of an international adoption agency, I expose the bare bones of this type of institution. Ethical agencies don't intentionally shroud themselves in mystery; they just don't have time to explain all of their inner workings any more than a business corporation does. With preparation and education, you can legally adopt a child internationally, provided you survive the medical, social, and financial background checks and still retain your desire to adopt.

This book offers a proven, easy-to-follow method for understanding what an adoption agency does and does not do. The book is divided into three parts. Review Part I to learn how adoption agencies are set up.

First off, "adoption agency" is a misnomer. "Placement agency" would be more accurate. Here's what international adoption agencies actually do:

- Create and maintain a licensed nonprofit agency that operates according to current state, federal, and foreign adoption laws

- Prepare and educate clients in the science of international adoption

- Interview the prospective parents, inspect the home, review their supporting documents, and conduct a social evaluation, called a home study

Note: If a family resides in a state where the international adoption agency isn't licensed, a local agency can conduct the home study via a networking agreement.

Read Part II to assess the international component in these adoptions. The completion of an adoption hinges on the strength of the agency's staff, both here and abroad. This is what the agency does:

- Travels abroad to form child-placing agreements with government entities

- Trains staff abroad to coordinate adoption services

- Facilitates child placement

Scrutinize Part III to dissect the intricacies of selecting, meeting, and adopting a child abroad. The agency

- shares the child's referral information with the adoptive parents;

- guides the adoptive parents throughout their stay abroad;

- provides emotional support for the family's initial adjustment;

- follows up with post-adoption supervisory visits and resources for a satisfactory family adjustment.

Here's what agencies don't do:

- Gather original and certified documents, such as birth certificates, for adoptive parents
- Control the governments and courts regarding referrals of children and their adoptions abroad
- Conduct the adoption, readoption, or reaffirmation of the adoption in adoptive parents' home state
- Assist with children's U.S. passports
- Apply for children's Social Security numbers

Anecdotes illustrating key issues are sprinkled throughout this book. Successful adoptions are the norm, thanks to the emotional maturity, mental and physical health, and financial stability of the majority of adoptive parents. These strengths enable them to adopt and to raise children successfully. The families see their children as precious gifts and as benefits to their entire community.

International adoption is a highly complex venture. It's been said that once the mind has been stretched by new information and a healthy dose of skepticism, it can never return to its original size. Learning what goes on inside an agency will ease your journey through the adoption process. Understanding the key points of the Hague Convention will strengthen your ability to follow the adoption process at a higher level. Once this book has been studied cover to cover, you will be a better educated, more discriminating, and more understanding client…or you may decide that international adoption is not for you.

HOW TO GET THE MOST OUT OF THIS BOOK

- Read it and educate yourself *before* you find a child to adopt.
- Refer to it while reviewing the literature from adoption agencies.
- Learn how to deal with a child's formal referral information.
- Realize that things change. If you plan to adopt in a few years, rather than now, the agency you're interested in, as well as the country from which you wish to adopt, may no longer be involved in international adoption.

PART I
International Adoption

1

What an International Adoption Agency Does

Do you want to do something beautiful for God?
There is a person who needs you. This is your chance.

—Mother Teresa

Some folks spend more time researching the purchase of a car than they do studying the process of adopting a child. They bond with a child or photo without knowing that their state regulations, the rules of the U.S. Citizenship and Immigration Service (CIS), and the laws and procedures of the foreign country must be adhered to and coordinated. They often hope to bypass international adoption agencies. This is where frustration, heartbreak, and expensive immigration attorneys come in.

- **Tip**: If you want to adopt, find an ethical agency first. Then find a child. (Special-needs and older children may be the exception.)

Experienced agencies are not an impediment to this complex process, but a source of know-how. The agency's social workers are not nearly as judgmental as you might think. Instead, they're eager to help you adopt. They're required to review your supporting documents, interview you, inspect your home, and write a social evaluation (home study) that presents you in the best possible light to CIS, the court abroad, and in a few states like Minnesota, to the state welfare agency.

Why does this seem so intimidating to the average American?

- **Tip**: You don't have to have a spotless life or a spotless house.

This book is based on the experiences of the staff of Los Niños International Adoption Center (LNI), which was established in 1981 by my husband, Heino R. Erichsen, MA, and me. The agency was modeled after the highly ethical Holt International Children's Services, which was founded in 1956. A medium-sized agency with a staff of around a dozen, LNI places around one hundred children a year. The majority of agencies are similar in size; other agencies may only have one or two workers. Large agencies have fifty to one hundred employees, who conduct domestic adoption programs in addition to foreign ones, foster care, refugee programs, and a host of other social-service projects. Regardless of size, reputable agencies follow the same basic pattern and provide similar services for international adoptions. Full-time employees must pass background checks and meet minimum degree and experience requirements.

The staff of a typical agency is made up of several positions:

- Executive director
- Director of international program development and public policy (the Hague Convention)
- Director of communications
- Supervisor of social work
- Program director
- Social worker(s)
- International case worker(s)
- Financial assistant/administrative assistant(s)

When we opened LNI in 1981, fifty international adoption agencies existed in the United States. At this writing (February 2006), around three thousand such agencies exist, with more opening every year. For the first twenty years, LNI didn't need to advertise. We focused on laying the groundwork abroad, since our clients arrived by word of mouth. Sometimes solo and sometimes with the family, Heino visited nearly every Latin American country and made child-placing agreements with most of them. Ten years after we founded the agency, he traveled extensively in Asia and Eastern Europe, with the same goal in mind. He avoided nations under Muslim rule, because they did not appear to have adoption laws. Sandwiched among Heino's adoption trips abroad were meetings at the U.S. State Department and in the Hague, Holland, to participate in the Hague Convention on the Protection of Children and Cooperation in Respect of

Intercountry Adoption. Drafts for the treaty were published in 1991. The text for the treaty concluded in 1993. Most countries ratified and implemented the treaty soon after that. But the United States was still holding off ratification in 2006.

The Hague Convention met with a lot of resistance from a slew of adoption agencies. A few of the agencies did not want to open their files and finances to inspection. But the biggest concern for most of them was that the proposed accreditation process might be prohibitively expensive and that the addition of another bureaucracy would slow down the adoption process. Yet the advantages far outweigh the disadvantages for children, as well as ethical agencies and their clients. To review the text of the convention, visit www.hcch.net.

The goals of the treaty are beneficial and far-reaching:

- Require national adoption laws in countries where none exist, such as the United States of America

- Accredit adoption agencies

- Mandate international adoptive-parent training

- Establish a standard procedure for adoption

- Create the concept of a central authority to supervise documentation on adoptable children, birth parents, and adoptive parents

- Decree that the abduction, exploitation, sale, or trafficking of children is a criminal act

For half a century, the United States, which receives the most adoptive children from abroad, has had no national adoption law, no central authority, and not nearly enough cohesion between state and federal agencies. International adoptions were uncontrolled. There were no effective safeguards in place for the adoptive parents or the adopted children. Illegal and inhumane practices broke the hearts of a lot of children, biological parents, and adoptive parents. These illegal activities grabbed the attention of the media, and international adoption gained a bad reputation due to the haphazard way it was conducted—and the loopholes that allowed criminals to operate.

Fifty years after the Holts opened the first international agency, the regulations for the Hague Convention on the Protection of Children and Cooperation in Respect of Intercountry Adoption were finally issued and readied for ratification and implementation by the United States of America.

2

Birthing an Agency

The births of all things are weak and tender, and therefore,
our eyes should be intent on beginnings.

—Michel Eyquem Montaigne

Before we begin, a little history is in order. International adoption began with the missionary zeal of Harry Holt, a retired lumber baron in Oregon. In the mid-1950s, after the Korean War, Harry and his wife, Bertha, saw a film about Amerasian children in Korean orphanages. The children were desperately in need of help. Harry and Bertha sent money and clothes, but that didn't feel like enough. Then the Holts came to an inspired realization: those children needed families. They could open their home to at least eight.

The Holts decided to adopt, but soon learned it would be impossible...unless they could get both houses of Congress to pass a special law. "Then that's what we'll do," Bertha said, and she moved ahead on faith. The couple founded Holt International Children's Services using their personal funds. From the beginning, they emphasized that homes should be sought for children within the country of origin before considering an international adoption. But despite Korea's efforts to find the children's relatives and set up foster homes, thousands of children still needed parents. By the early 1970s, the Holts' agency grew from a mom-and-pop organization to the largest international adoption agency in the United States. By then the agency was also placing children orphaned by the war in Vietnam. Holt networked with agencies in every state in order to place all of the Korean children that needed families.

Harry and Bertha Holt's adoption of Korean children was revolutionary in several respects. Even as their example showed that a family's love can transcend the barriers of race and nationality, their determination demonstrated that new laws can be forged. For example, the U.S. Immigration and Naturalization Services (INS, now called CIS, for Citizenship and Immigration Service) slowly improved its processing of orphans. Today, when both parents have visited the child abroad prior to or during the adoption, the child is an automatic citizen upon arrival at a U.S. port of entry.

Fast-forward twenty years from when the Holts adopted. Heino and I were already parents of three biological sons, Joergen, Arthur, and Kirk, when we adopted twin infant daughters, Rosana and Tatiana, at an adoption agency in Colombia in the seventies. A Colombian colleague had told me about the needy children in her country: a fourteen-year civil war had created thousands of abandoned babies and children. On a trip home, she visited an adoption agency, Casa de la Madre y el Niño, on our behalf and received the twin's referrals for us much earlier than we expected. But we weren't prepared with the right documents and forms. The U.S. Immigration and Naturalization Service wasn't ready either; it had never processed an orphan petition for the Western Hemisphere. Its experience lay in the Eastern Hemisphere, with Korean and Vietnamese petitions. Heino explained the situation to Minnesota Senator Hubert Humphrey and met with INS to review its regulations on the Western Hemisphere. We finally obtained approval to proceed. Two months later, we flew to Bogota to meet our beautiful babies in a different world. While we appreciated Colombia's wondrous culture, we were shocked and dismayed at the sight of thousands of children living on the streets.

As we departed, the director of the Colombian agency pressed the photos of eight orphans into Heino's hand. "Please find good parents for them," she said.

I barely heard her. With my arms full of babies, blankets, and bottles, I was thinking about how I would manage when I got home. With only nine months between our biological baby and our two-month-old infants, I needed to ratchet up my efficiency and find some women to help me. Opening an adoption agency was the furthest thing from my mind.

Fortunately Heino was game and wasted no time in calling the adoption agencies in Minnesota about these orphans, who ranged in age from three to eight years old. Thanks to the agencies' cooperation, prospective parents were quickly found for all of the children.

But after the agencies found potential parents, we were in the unique position of feeling some responsibility for the completion of their adoptions. Heino and I were each cast in the roles of hesitant educator and adoption coordinator. We had jumped into adoption literally blindfolded and could hardly call ourselves experts. Yet we felt compelled to prepare couples for the care and adoption of a child in exotic surroundings and a language most of them didn't speak. The thrill of seeing proud couples come home with their mission—becoming the parents of a beautiful Latin American child—accomplished gave rise to a lifetime commitment. We spent the next six years volunteering for OURS (Organization for a United Response) and for adoption agencies in Minnesota, and writing our first book, *Gamines: How to Adopt in Latin America,* which was published in 1981. Through guidance, research, and writing, we paved the way for thousands of couples and singles to adopt homeless children south of the border.

When our children started elementary school in 1981, we went to school and graduated with master's degrees in human development, specializing in international adoption sources. The concept of starting an adoption agency developed slowly. Unlike the Holts, we were not independently wealthy. What we had instead was the benefit of observing other adoption agencies with international programs prior to founding one. Eight years after we adopted the twins, Heino came up with a name, Los Niños International Aid and Adoption Center (LNI), and obtained nonprofit corporation status, as well as a license for the agency in Minnesota.

We started small, with limited personal funds. Some agencies obtain grants from public and private sectors or churches to get started, but Heino didn't want to be dependent on these sources; they can dry up and leave you stranded. A year later, we moved to Texas, a state where few children from abroad had immigrated (in comparison to Minnesota, where thousands had). We were the first to establish a U.S.-based international adoption agency in Texas. In 1983 we took our children back to Colombia to introduce our agency to the Colombian national welfare department, Instituto Colombiano de Bienestar Familiar, and the Colombian adoption agencies in Bogota. At one of them, our family met nine-year-old Omar, a former street child, and were captivated by his genuine goodness and charm. Heino went back to emigrate him three months later. Our family felt complete.

When Heino began to establish the agency, he had no thoughts about its growth. Like a newborn baby, the agency took on a character of its own and slowly developed and matured. Heino didn't think big; foresee an impressive building or a multilevel staff. While I was focused on adoptive-parent preparation and education, his goal was to find homes for the children. At that time, most existing social-service agencies were either faith-based or private agencies that had carried out adoption services for a long time. One of them was Children's Home Society (CHS) of Minnesota, which went back a hundred years to the days of the "Orphan Train," when homeless children from the industrial cities of the East Coast were put on trains to the Midwest to find parents for them.

Back when we contacted CHS for a home study (social evaluation) in order to adopt from Colombia, it was placing Korean and Vietnamese orphans. Asian children were brought to the United States by volunteers, placed with their parents at the airport, and formally adopted six months later. Heino and I volunteered for CHS after we pioneered adoption in Colombia. We introduced that nation as a new source of children to CHS clients and helped coordinate the adoptions. Over the next six years, we listened and learned from the agency.

One of the many important facts Heino gleaned was that it would be best for our new agency to obtain a child-placing license from our state and nonprofit status from the Internal Revenue Service.

The latter is known as 501(c)(3) status. It was cumbersome to obtain while we formed the adoption agency, but vital. Although obtaining this status took a lot of time and effort, Heino and I knew there were needy children awaiting adoption in Latin America. While we were in Colombia, we had seen a lot of children waiting for families at the agency. We also saw children begging on the streets or performing backbreaking labor, carrying loads far too heavy for their young bodies. Since we were older and had adopted transracially, we agreed that our new agency would not attempt to match children racially with prospective parents. We would accept potential parents of all races, creeds, and colors, as well as singles and couples up to sixty years old or older, depending on the minimum and maximum age requirements of the foreign countries.

Eight years after we adopted, LNI received its 501(c)(3) approval from the Internal Revenue Service and a license in the state of Minnesota. The agency took root and grew like a kudzu vine. Heino and I worked out of our home with a licensed social worker. A job offer for Heino in Austin, Texas, gave him the opportunity to be closer to the potential sources in Latin America. Working under Minnesota license as a "foreign" agency (the Texas term for an out-of-state licensed entity), Heino and I applied for a Texas child-placing license. He soon resigned from his Austin job to travel to countries where he knew the laws permitted the international adoption of children. We had done extensive research in every country in Central and South America.

Here again he set up an office at home. On Heino's first day in his new job, nine-year-old Tatiana came to him with concerned look in her dark brown eyes and said, "Are you sick, Daddy? Shouldn't you be at work?" When Heino told her he would be working at home, she said, "That's great! Why don't we all stay home?" But I didn't think I could homeschool the children and do my social-work job all at the same time. So the kids went to school, and we stayed home during the first year of operation.

We selected our first board of directors from the community. This board included a medical doctor and a lawyer.

Few international adoptions had occurred in Texas. By contrast Minnesotan families had welcomed thousands of children from Korea and from Vietnam. Now that we lived in Texas, we bordered Mexico and were much closer to all of Latin America. Heino and I had taken Spanish lessons and had a basic understanding of the cultures and languages south of our border. We had befriended local Colombian consuls and American visa officers in Colombia who encouraged us to help the children. (Colombia placed thousands of babies internationally until 2004, when their government put several mandates into effect. Children over seven were given first priority for adoption processing, and birth mothers were instructed to keep their babies, rather than relinquish them for adoption.)

Heino's blueprint for success abroad was to visit the government authorities, get their approval, and hire bilingual representatives in that country to coordinate adoptions. From research he knew of the need in Chile, which had gone through an overthrow of the elected government. After visiting the agencies in Colombia, he traveled to Chile, visited attorneys listed with the American embassy in Santiago, and hired the people we needed. This meant performing the difficult trick of supervising employees from a distance. Heino expected these representatives to secure all of the available referral information on an appropriate child and send it to us for review, then handle all the steps of the adoption before and during the prospective parent's arrival. During the adopter's stay in that country, our representatives were to serve as bilingual travel guides and problem solvers. All we needed was a guinea pig.

A single man appeared who was optimistic and flexible enough to deal with uncertainly and blatant negativity: Dr. Don, a podiatrist. Although he had never found the right woman to marry, he was desperate for a child to love and care for. No one, from his social worker to the folks at INS and the notary who signed his documents, believed we could place a child from Chile in the United States, especially not with a single man. Dr. Don called frequently to tell me about the mistrust he combated on a daily basis. Although his calls to immigration officials made him feel as though he were wasting their time, a personal visit made his application for an orphan visa a reality.

The immigration officer read his home study, leaned over her desk, and said, "So you're a podiatrist?"

"Yes, I am," the doctor replied.

The lady officer gave him an anguished look and said, "My feet are killing me. Could you tell me what I should do?"

As quickly as Dr. Don said, "I'd be glad to," she shucked off her shoes, and Dr. Don examined her feet. He gave her his opinion and recommended a podiatrist in her area. The lady was so pleased that she helped him fill out his application without further ado. The doctor went back to his office and quickly set up a nursery where his enthusiastic staff could help care for the baby. Shortly thereafter he was assigned a cute eighteen-month-old boy named Rico. Dr. Don traveled to Chile and brought the child home.

"Everything went as smooth as silk, and Rico is as cute as a button," the proud new father announced over the phone. Rico was the first of over a hundred Chilean babies to find homes in the United States through our agency. (Later on the Chilean welfare system decided that only children over four years of age could be placed abroad.)

The next country Heino visited was Honduras, one of the poorest countries of Central America. He met a lawyer who eventually became the attorney general. The lawyer had a flair and a machismo that no one who met him ever forgot. At one point, Heino and I went to visit him in Tegucigalpa, Honduras, when criminals he had sent to prison had been released and were after him. He sat with us in a restaurant with plate-glass windows, his back to the door. "I'm not afraid of them," he said, and impressed us with his daring. When we left the restaurant, he had a quick huddle with his armed bodyguard—who, we realized, had been standing outside the whole time.

Over the next ten years, that lawyer helped find homes for Honduran children. Then, all of a sudden, anti-adoption forces brought the adoptions to a standstill that continues even as I write this book.

Word of the availability of Latin American children spread. Without ever advertising, we had an unanticipated influx of clients. In our home office, we needed more space and employees. Heino moved the office several times in search of adequate space. We hired a Spanish-speaking office manager, a secretary, and an international case worker (which was not difficult in Austin, which was nearly 50 percent Latino). Working with our board of directors, we drew up our first bylaws. Shortly after that, Heino formalized our first networking agreements with adoption agencies for the waiting children.

Heino had no concrete thoughts about the future of the agency, even after our second trip to Colombia to forge agreements with the adoption agencies there. But he knew that in order to keep on top of the international situation, we needed to stay in the loop. On behalf of the agency, Heino joined two umbrella organizations: Joint Council on International Children's Services and the National Council for Adoption, both of which are located in Washington DC. We met all of the agencies that we had communicated with for so many years, attended workshops, and pooled information.

Many other agencies were competing with us by then, partly because we had freely given away our information on the sources and procedures. We were more interested in seeing children find loving homes than in handling every case ourselves. The competition just made Heino's travels longer, more frequent, and more widespread. He opened programs in Peru, Bolivia, Paraguay, Ecuador, and Guatemala, and even in El Salvador, which was then in the midst of a bloody civil war. As a former soldier, he told me that his nerves were on edge the whole time he was in the capital city of San Salvador. The sound of all the gunfire gave him flashbacks. We had second thoughts about the program, since we feared for our clients. Fortunately Heino was able to arrange proxy adoptions and find Salvadorians willing to bring the children to their new parents in the United States.

Cataclysmic political events continued to unfold. In just one month in 1992, I witnessed inexplicable situations in two very different capital cities: Panama City, Panama, and Bucharest, Romania. Our children accompanied us as we set up an adoption program with the Panamanian government and toured the area. On our last day, when the driver heard we were involved in adoption, he took us through the city slum. Unpainted, rickety, two-story Victorian-style houses lined dark, narrow, potholed streets. Yet our family delighted in the antics of the happy, playful children who ran up to the van and grinned. A group of ragged little boys even posed for pictures when they noticed that our girls had a camera.

A few weeks later, the United States invaded Panama City in order to rid the country of dictator Manuel Noriega, in Operation Just Cause. All six of us stared at the television that night in disbelief: U.S. Air Force jets were bombing the slum! In minutes the entire area was engulfed in flames. "I hope the kids got out in time," said a teary-eyed Rosana. She expressed what all of us were feeling as we wiped our tears away.

That same month, the dictatorship of Ceausescu in Romania collapsed. This was the first crack in the Iron Curtain. Reports of the former dictator's harsh edicts seemed outlandish. One such order, for each woman to have five children, caused a sharp increase in births but no provision for improvement in the standard of living. A national television network in the United States traveled to Romania to produce a documentary on the orphanages in Romania. They discovered thousands of pitifully malnourished, neglected children in orphanages. The program, "Shame of a Nation," tore at American heartstrings. The fact that the majority of the children were white awoke deep parental feelings. Adoption agencies were bombarded with calls from couples who wanted to know how to rescue a Romanian child from an orphanage. Television had set off the greatest child-saving mission in U.S. history. Heino was soon on the plane to Bucharest to explore an adoption program—the first in Eastern Europe.

Then, unexpectedly, China invited Westerners inside their orphanages. Heino and I traveled there to follow the progress of our first two families. Countries formerly under Soviet control followed Romania in a domino effect, beginning with Russia. However, in the case of Vietnam, Heino waited to start an adoption program until President Clinton's embargo was lifted. In a Northern province, we built an orphanage and placed 115 babies and children before the government decided to reorganize and create a central authority. Three years later, our country signed an agreement with Vietnam, and in February 2006, Heino was on a plane again to develop a new adoption program under Vietnam's directives.

Heino realized long ago that incessant travel is a necessity for opening and sustaining adoption programs. In 2005, Heino and I traveled to Portuguese-speaking Brazil. This was a country he had missed on his initial pioneering trips to Latin America. Larger in square miles than the United States, Brazil has a much greater number of homeless children. In Sao Paulo, we met with lawyers and adoption officials to develop a new adoption program.

As an accountant, Heino had learned that pioneering trips are financially risky but worth taking. Only time can tell whether a new adoption program will come to fruition and improve the lives of homeless children…or fail miserably if the majority of prospective adoptive parents find the program unacceptable. The requirements for adoptive parents might be too rigid, the wait too long, or the expenses too high in comparison with other countries. And few potential adopters want to be the first. So we must always wait for prospective adopters like the unflappable Dr. Don, who adopted little Rico in Chile. The cycle continues.

Heino realized that he had thought small and had won big. He could see the beneficial effects of his new job in our own family. And he was finally able to employ his skills in languages, geography, international politics, travel, management, and accounting. Suddenly he had a sense of meaning and purpose that translated itself into the happy new families that came to visit. On a scale of one to ten, one being the lowest and ten the highest, Heino rated his job satisfaction as a ten.

- **Tip:** Pick an adoption agency that travels to the countries where they place children. An agency that stays at home risks being uninformed about the processes and procedures in their programs.

Heino's final word about the process can be summed up easily. Only one thing is constant in international adoption: change!

3

Marketing Adoption Services

My wish is that children be treated as people, and not as property; that their rights as human beings on the planet, to food, shelter, education and health, be taken seriously.

—Oprah Winfrey

If you're thinking about adopting abroad this year, you'll join over twenty thousand others who hope to do the same. Agencies that think big hire marketing firms to design every aspect of their advertising campaigns and spend hundreds of thousands of dollars to get their message out. In order to cater to the emotional needs of prospective parents, information on the emotional and physical needs of institutionalized children is usually downplayed until you apply.

The pitfall for prospective parents is in trying to pick a trustworthy agency that will fulfill their dreams. When folks Google "international adoption agencies," they're overwhelmed by the magnitude of the advertising. They can click on gorgeous Web sites, watch glorious DVDs, and review glossy literature. This strongly appeals to potential parents who carry the picture of a certain type of child in their heads.

If you visit fifty Web sites, you'll see a huge difference in presentation. The agencies have made things easier by including an order form or their Web sites so that you can e-mail a request for information. With time and patience, you can send for fifty information packets. If you're pressed for time, visit Rainbowkids.com or a similar site and order your fifty packets from there—with one stroke of a key. And you can get your literature e-mailed or sent by U.S. post. (Just don't fall in love with a child who is pictured; you need to first make certain the agency offering the child is ethical.)

From the moment you type in your name, you are in a preadoptive category, and your contact information is entered into a database. Prepare yourself for a barrage of follow-up calls, invitations to seminars, postcards, newsletters, and magazines.

When you see a full-page ad in a national magazine, know that it probably cost the agency around ten thousand dollars for the concept and layout and around twenty thousand dollars for the ad itself. Adoption magazines are more reasonable; they charge about $1,000 for a full-page ad per issue. That's still too much for smaller agencies.

Web sites like Rainbowkids.com and AdoptiveFamilies.com charge the agencies for listings, as do a myriad of hard-copy adoption directories. Adoption fairs, usually sponsored by adoptive-parent groups, are held around the country. They charge the agency for a booth and for listing their names in the fair's brochures. In order to compete at these fairs, adoption agencies must capture attention with aesthetic attractions like impressive table displays and banners featuring pictures of beautiful babies. The banners and displays cost hundreds of dollars. Agencies must also find folks to man the booth, answer questions, and distribute the literature.

Once you gather fifty folders and lay them out, you'll find extremes in presentations: at the top end, gorgeous baby photos printed on textured covers; at the low end, construction-paper folders filled with a mess of photocopied literature.

But does the quality of the literature, Web site, and follow-up guarantee excellent service when you become a client? Not necessarily. The agency's administrators are responsible for the presentation and marketing—as is its staff—but you seldom get to know these folks until quite a bit later. However, you will depend on these people to hold your hand while they guide you through the preadoption steps. This is why it's important to contact agencies in your city or state first. When you consider that you'll have a personal relationship with the agency for several years, it makes sense to get to know these people and to be able to visit when your paperwork is snarled, when problems surface, or when you need to see your social worker for emotional support.

As it stands, about half of our clients are Texas residents. Families in our neighborhood in The Woodlands sometimes adopt through out-of-state agencies, and our agency welcomes families from other states. Only in America does a potential client have so many choices.

- **Tip:** If you're in the information-gathering phase, start a spreadsheet to keep track of the agencies' programs, waiting times, and fees, the number of adoption trips required, how long you must stay abroad, and an estimate of the hidden costs of living abroad for anywhere from several days to several months while you wait for the child's final adoption decree.

(The exact time you'll need to stay depends on the country's policy; most countries require one or both parents to make at least a brief trip to complete an adoption.)

When you've whittled the best agencies down to three, call each one. Keep track of their response time. Arrange for a personal consultation by phone or in person. Prior to the appointment, write up a list of questions. That way you'll hear what you need to know, rather than a spiel on the benefits of adopting from their agency. Some of your first questions should be

- Have the parental rights been terminated in court before a child is referred to me?
- Will I get full medical and social information on the child?
- Does your agency work directly with their own representatives abroad, or does your agency piggyback by working through another agency with representatives abroad?
- What is your ratio of staff to clients in the program that interests me?
- Do you have a backup program that would also be open to me, considering my age, marital status, number of prior marriages, and so on?
- What services do you provide after I am home?
- Who can I call if we need help?
- Can you arrange for me to talk to parents who have already adopted through your agency? I'm interested in adopting a child in _____.

The last bulleted point will help you fill in the expense gaps on your spreadsheet. Nailing down the cost is impossible using only your stack of adoption packets. Agencies use different terminology, lump expenses together, and let you know that certain expenses are not included, such as travel costs and immigration fees. As you talk to families, ask them about the overall experience and about the fees paid. You need to know!

Information on adoption financing is available in a booklet titled *You Can Afford Adoption.* It's available through A Mother's Charm at www.motherscharm.com. In their recent electronic newsletter, the authors estimated that the total cost of an international adoption is $28,000. It's paid in increments.

Depending on the country you choose, your final total will also be affected by the agency's operating costs, which are a lot higher in some states, such as New York and California. Ask the agencies to break down their fee structure.

INTERNATIONAL ADOPTION EXPENSES*	
Application Processing Fee	$500 to $1,000
Home Study (Social Evaluation)	$1,000 to $3,000
Post-adoption Study	$1,000 to $3,000
Agency Service Fee	$5,000 to $8,000
Specific Country Adoption Fee	$5,000 to $20,000**
Citizenship and Immigration Service Fees	$1,000

*Airfare and living expenses abroad not included. Consult a travel agency, travel book, and airline Web sites for estimates.

**With China the lowest and Guatemala and Russia the highest

Prior to your visit, ask the agencies to send you a copy of their agency agreement (or client contract). What you'll find is that the agency protects itself, and that you must be ready to take some risks. Ask for a sample placement agreement that you will sign when you accept a child's referral as well. This agreement outlines the possible emotional, mental, and physical problems a child might have when placed with you or soon afterward. These two documents are eye-openers. Faced with all the risks, prospective parents have been known to cancel their adoption plans! But most persevere, knowing that getting involved with another human being, adult or child, can be financially and emotionally risky.

Go to adoption seminars, especially if the agencies hold them in their offices. You'll get to meet the staff and see how well the agency is organized. You'll also get to meet families who have recently adopted and who will share their experiences.

Seminars are beneficial to prospective adoptive parents but can be risky for adoption agencies. For example, weeks before the event, press releases are sent out. Public radio is the most effective, but it charges hefty advertising fee. Other forms of media don't charge nonprofit agencies…but we don't know whether they'll run the press releases either. We incur costs for printing literature and for renting space at locations other than our office. Our goal is provide useful adoption information to prospective adoptive parents. The typical adoptive parents are polite and cooperative, and—judging by their evaluation forms—appreciative of our efforts. We keep seminars short, with an hour for the how-to, after which we give the floor to recently returned adoptive families who bring their children and talk about their experiences for the second hour. While most singles and couples who attend already have a general understanding of the process, walk-ins can disrupt the proceedings—or try to.

The most galling and annoying guests we have, though, are the ones who want to get into the "business." They study our literature and listen to our program, then wait until our backs are turned to try to persuade our guests to dump us and use their services instead.

No one could ever top the audacity of a foreign national who had decided to open an adoption agency in Texas. She didn't come inside; instead she stood in the parking lot of the church we had rented for an afternoon workshop. As people were leaving, she told them to use her new agency instead of ours and distributed her printed literature stating she had an MSW (a master's degree in social work). A check with the Department of Licensing and Regulations proved that she didn't. Nor did she even have an agency license at that point. I called her about it; she told me she had such a degree in her country. If so, it was not the same as a master's degree used in social work here. I still wonder what other unethical methods she used to get ahead.

- **TIP:** Check the credentials of the agencies that interest you. Don't take it from them; do your research. The Hague regulations provide an important benefit in this area. Agencies licensed under the Hague regulations will have proved their status through a lengthy review process.

An outspoken lady in a faux fur coat attended one of our seminars. On closer examination, her bright red lipstick seemed to be smeared across her face. She was loud and full of questions. A reporter for the *Dallas Morning News* sitting next to me said, "She's drunk." The room was crowded. For a few moments, I mulled over what to do as the woman continued to monopolize the seminar with repetitive questions. I got two employees to escort her out the door when I called a break and the audience was milling around. No one seemed to notice.

At another seminar, an eccentric, white-haired man in his sixties showed up, dressed like Crocodile Dundee. He told us he was a "trust-fund baby" and wanted a child only so his money wouldn't go to the government when he died. While we talked, my daughter was decorating a table and arranging snacks on it for the seminar. She had just put the finishing touches on when Mr. Eccentric piled up a plate with half of the food and gobbled it down. On our way out, we found him napping on our lawn.

Then, of course, there are the husbands who don't want to be there in the first place. They either fall asleep or demand a full accounting of the expenses, no matter how much time it takes away from our planned program. It's highly unlikely that such couples will ever follow through.

When you attend a seminar, keep an open mind. Prepare yourself to hear both the joys of adoption and the possible risks. Ask questions as appropriate, but reserve highly personal or detailed questions for staff after the presentation is through.

Once you choose an agency, here's the breakdown of how long it takes just to get ready for the referral of a child: application, one week; gathering documentation and obtaining a social evaluation or home study, eight weeks; and preparation of the documents for the court abroad, eight weeks. 1+8+8=17 weeks, or approximately four months.

At the same time, you must coordinate these efforts at the nearest U.S. Citizenship and Immigration Service (CIS) office. You must fill out and send in a form, along with a fee payment and the documents that are listed on said form. Visit uscis.gov/graphics/formsfee/index.htm and print out the I-600A "Advance Processing of an Orphan Petition." If you file the aforesaid items at the U.S. Citizenship and Immigration office when you start your home study, CIS will contact you for a fingerprint appointment and send them to the FBI for clearance. These early steps may result in CIS sending you its approval, called the I-171H, while you're still preparing your documents for the court abroad. However, some CIS offices, such as the one in Boston, insist that people submit the I-600A with a completed home study report.

- **Tip:** Thinking ahead with the I-600A saves time in states where advance filing is permitted. The resultant I-171H is a required part of documentation for the adoption abroad in most countries and a necessity for the immigration of your child.

Depending on the country you intend to adopt from, you will wait for a few months to a year or more for the referral of a child, or an invitation to travel abroad to select a child. Then all the preadoption paperwork you've done will come to fruition, and there shouldn't be any glitches with the child's adoption and immigration—unless, of course, the country of the child's birth changes its requirements, requiring that some of your documents be redone! You can also expect to redo some documents that may be expired after six or twelve months.

Unfortunately a lot of prospective adoptive parents are too anxious to stick with the cautious procedure I suggest. Adoption marketers have a field day on the

Internet with them. "Thinking about adoption? Visit our photo listings of children." This is similar to real estate photo listings, but with an important difference: when the house goes off the market, it will no longer be posted, but this is not true of pretty little girls and handsome little boys. Their pictures are often a come-on.

Jody Clark (not her real name) learned this the hard way. She was used to getting what she wanted when she wanted it. Tall and slim, she strode into our office with such high energy and determination that sparks seemed to fly. She was an attractive businesswoman with a stylish, shiny black bob, and she was dressed for success. "I've got my heart set on this child." she said. She had done exactly what we tell our clients not to do: she had gotten attached to a picture on the Internet, a two-year-old girl in Kazakhstan. "This is the perfect child for me, I just know it."

Yet all Jody really had was the child's first name and the name of the agency that advertised her. She knew nothing about the lengthy procedures, the long stay in the child's country, the child's state of health, or whether the child was even legally available.

Jody had called the agency that posted the girl on the Internet, and was told that the child was still available. "Send us $3,500 immediately, and we'll put a hold on her," the agency told her. They also indicated that she should call a local agency in order to obtain a written social evaluation (home study) for the court in the child's region. Since we were in her neighborhood, Jody came to our office for a preliminary consultation. We told her we could help her if she would also consider adopting through our own program in the same country if this child's adoption did not materialize. She agreed. She brought her husband to our next seminar. They sounded as if they were both on board.

But Jody had put the cart before the horse. At this point, we hadn't even approved her application. I had a lot of concerns, because she was so impatient. She called a week later to say the child was no longer available, yet she had a long chat with our social worker. Jody had discovered that the agency she found on the Internet piggybacked on an agency that had a direct program in the child's country. Jody was more confused than ever, but she said a friend who traveled on business to that country would try to visit the child. In the meantime, Jody was pressuring the agency to whom she had paid $3,500. When she called them a few weeks later, they told her the child was available again. Jody relayed this information to us and said she wanted her application fee back, because she had found an independent social worker who would write her home study more cheaply and quickly than we could. A year later, I bumped into Jody at the mall. She told me she had finally given up and didn't believe anything the agency told her anymore, and that a lawyer was trying to get her money back.

Summer camps for Eastern European children follow a similar pattern. This is rather like a marketing tool some agencies use to place children. The United States allows the agencies to apply to CIS for temporary tourist visas for the children to live with an American family for two to four weeks. Orphanage directors agree to let them go, and the staff gets a chance to relax. While the majority of older children have found new parents that they wouldn't have otherwise, some children have later said they didn't want to come here or that they didn't want to be adopted.

The adoption agencies place the children with volunteer foster parents. The fact that some of the foster homes are not fully approved under state standards by a social worker should make any thinking person nervous. But most of the time, the foster families are moral and responsible. They usually decide they want to adopt the child, even though they have no idea whether the child is legally free for adoption, how the adoption process works, the trips and length of stay abroad, or the costs. Rather than a reasoned decision, it's an emotional one. At the end of the two-to four-week "camp," the CIS regulations require that children be returned to their homeland, go back to the orphanage, and wait for their prospective adoptive parents (who may or may not qualify to adopt them). If all goes well, the potential parents qualify to adopt and show up in the foreign court to adopt. The children come back on orphan visas and are granted automatic citizenship.

Summer camp can be fraught with peril for some children. One of them was jittery four-year-old Ika, who was ejected from three foster homes in the United States before one of our approved families heard of her plight. These were experienced parents who understood it would take a long time for Ika to get over the emotional traumas that began in her birth country. Although summer camp was a bumpy ride for Ika, it finally gave her a patient, loving family.

Sandra Carlson, a licensed certified social worker, added her thoughts here with, "Just a note about these summer camps. I have a lot of concern for the children who want to live here and have been introduced to a better way of life—and then no one wants to adopt them. This seems inhuman to me."

Author's note: On my last trip to Russia, I proposed that summer camps be held at Lake Baikal, where everyone, including the orphanage staff, could get a vacation, and prospective adoptive parents could volunteer their talents while they got to know the children. I was told it was a good idea, but I doubt it was ever implemented.

Several lessons are to be learned here by prospective adoptive parents and agencies:

- Don't look for children on the Internet.

- Don't pick out a summer-camp child unless you are completely prepared, as described in the next chapter.

- Believe that your agency will find the appropriate child when you are paperwork ready, approved by U.S. immigration officials, and mentally and financially prepared to adopt.

- If the child is over ten, make certain the child wants to be adopted.

- If possible find an agency in your state, and preferably in your city, with a suitable adoption program in the country from which you wish to adopt—or at least a good home study/post-adoption "local service agency" that has experience with helping families through the ups and downs of the international adoption process. (You can use an out-of-state agency to place a child if you prefer its programs, but the home study must be done in your home state.)

4

Addressing Contracts and Agreements

Litigation—that machine which a man enters as a pig and leaves as a sausage.

—Ambrose Bierce, *The Devil's Dictionary*

I'll never forget the first time I was served papers. My secretary came to tell me in whispers what was up. I peeked around my door and saw a huge good ol' Texas country boy playing with an old-fashioned sock monkey I'd made. I quickly dialed our lawyer. "Go ahead and take the documents; he'll keep coming back until you do," was his advice.

With a fluttering heart, I took the envelope from the process server, who looked hopefully at me and said, "I used to have a monkey like this, but I can't find it. Will you make me another one?" I mumbled something about being too busy and hoped he would leave, so I could read the bad news he brought. Under my breath, I muttered, "What nerve!"

"You are being sued," the first sentence on the top sheet of papers declared. I sat down to read a long preamble that stated I was "a danger to the community." My husband and the board of directors were also named in this suit. Compensation of a million dollars was demanded by a family who had used our services—the husband, wife, and their two biological children—for their anxiety and loss of sleep during the year Elena was part of their family. The couple claimed fraud.

The couple had had an approved home study when they saw a picture in our newsletter of an eleven-year-old girl. They requested her medical and social information before they visited her in Guatemala. They told the authorities there they wanted to adopt her. After the adoption was finalized several months later, the parents returned to emigrate her.

The state, as well as the Hague Convention, requires adoption agencies to carry liability insurance. We were insured, but I didn't feel as if the suit were justified.

When the child first arrived, my social worker and I had spent many fruitless conversations with the adoptive mother, but we were unable to convince her that the child should not immediately be placed in elementary school with her age group. The child had had less than a year of education in a different language.

The adoptive mother's expectations pushed the child into rebellion. The adoptive mother and her husband did not notify us when they sent their daughter out-of-state to a residential treatment center. Then, six months later, when their insurance ran out, they had to bring her home. The father immediately called me to demand money for another residential treatment center. We had no funds for this. I told him no and said that what they really needed was family counseling.

In cases like this, some families want to blame the child and the agency instead of adjusting their level of tolerance in order to work out some compromises. I had hoped the family would give this child a break. Instead of that, they relinquished their parental rights to the state, so the child lived in various residences and foster homes until she was sixteen. Then she, along with some of the friends she had made at the foster home, ran away. Although the state tried to locate her until her eighteenth birthday, she was never found.

Another perturbed couple used a different approach. The Smiths (not their real names) cut to the chase and brought their lawyer directly to our office to demand their money back. The lawyer strode into our office, slammed his briefcase down on the conference table, and started insulting us, calling us baby sellers and worse. This childless couple had been studied and approved and had received referrals of two children that winter. They had traveled to Russia to adopt (at that time, only one trip was required). The boy was four, and his sister was two. Although every other adoptive couple brought toys and winter clothes to Russia for their new children, the Smiths brought nothing to keep their children warm and entertained.

After the adoption, they flew with the children for a chilly three-day stay in Moscow to obtain orphan visas. Cooped up in a small hotel room with nothing to do, the children squabbled; the older child punched the younger. The couple didn't know how to divert the children's attention and stop the bickering. They did not get in touch with us before they took the children back where they came from, even though they were the legal parents. We had done our job, but they couldn't do theirs. They had to sign relinquishment papers for dissolution in the same court. They did not get their money back, despite their lawyer's rants.

Problems rarely occur, but when they do, most prospective adoptive parents are mature enough to deal with them appropriately. Unfortunately a few adoptive parents have visited their long-anticipated child, only to find that he or she has a serious developmental delay or illness. This puts the prospective adopters in a quandary. Do they go ahead with the adoption, knowing they face the responsibility of the child's long-term treatment, or do they stop the adoption and feel guilt over leaving the child behind? In rare cases, a baby has died before the new parents could travel abroad to claim him.

We're in constant communication with these clients—to listen and to help them decide on the next steps. Every case is unique. While most of the parents want a another child as soon as possible, others need time to mourn. We respect their wishes and follow up when they are ready. An ethical agency should never force parents into a decision, only offer their professional advice.

Once I was asked to be an expert witness in a trial against another adoption agency. When I heard the facts, I couldn't do it, because it could have happened to any agency with an adoption program abroad. A preadoptive couple demanded a settlement from the agency for lost time and sleepless nights. The agency had been told over a period of nearly a year, as we all were, that the country in question would open again, and they relayed this information to their clients. During that long wait, most of the other couples had stuck with their agency but switched to another country. It was the right thing to do.

The litigation-minded couple continued to wait. Eventually the couple dropped the suit after they weighed their further time and stress versus the possibility of financial benefit. "It wasn't the money I was after, but an acknowledgment by the agency of our frustration at being strung along," the husband told me.

- **Tip:** Read your agency's contract or agreement carefully before applying and spending money. And read your agency's child-placing agreement, at the same time, even if it runs to twenty pages. (Some of them do.) If it makes you feel better, ask a lawyer to review these documents before you sign them.

One of our clients, Mary Reddy (not her real name) read her contract and called me to say that she was going to change it before she signed it. "It protects you, but it doesn't protect us," she said. "What if we want to sue you?" I gulped. After my breathing returned to normal, I told her she couldn't change it. Mary really surprised me, because she had never read any of our literature before. She was college-educated, but she couldn't manage to get her own documents together. She always needed hands-on help. She came to the office twice to spread out a mess of copies and documents and watch me sort through them. I filed the documents that were correct and gave her a customized list each time of what was missing. Now here she was considering a lawsuit before she even had her documents legalized.

Amazingly, the Reddys received the referral of a child just a week after the dossier of documents was finished. The wife claimed the quick turnaround didn't give her enough time to transfer the necessary funds out of her account. So we let the Reddys travel without paying the agency fee they owed us, because Mary promised to pay as soon as she got home. (We don't do that anymore.) She never paid us, or even the collection agency we eventually turned to. A year after she adopted, she called me. "Buddy is such a wonderful little boy that we want another one," she crowed. "Send me an application." I reminded her that she had never paid us. "Oh, that," she said. I guess she went to another agency.

PART II
Travel

5

Traveling Abroad (the Agency)

We must look on children in need not as problems but as individuals with potential…
I would hope we could find creative ways to draw out of our children the good
that is there in each of them.

—Archbishop Desmond Tutu

In meetings with adoption authorities, I noticed little difference in attitude between most state welfare authorities in the United States and the national welfare authorities in a lot of Latin and Eastern European countries. Few seemed to feel pressured to place the waiting children with adoptive parents.

We were too dependent on their goodwill to ask pointed questions, but I sometimes wonder if I should have. Had they ever been to an orphanage? Did they have any knowledge of the orphanage's detrimental effect on a child's growth and development? Did they understand that every month lost to their bureaucracy would probably require twice as much effort in catch-up growth and development for the child? My guess is that they had not and did not. Most of the government officials had not been educated in child development. Some had worked themselves up from positions as clerks and may not have had a choice about working in welfare. The higher the job, the more vigilance and politicking was necessary to keep it.

Visiting an orphanage is a heart-tugging event. I've toured them near and far, from Mexico to Mongolia. My feelings of impatience are always the same. The children are wards of the state, in essence—owned by the government. The possibility for an international adoption is in the hands of the welfare system. As we discovered in our travels, welfare authorities in some countries would rather see their children grow up in orphanages than be adopted by nonresidents. Whether this is a way to keep their jobs secure or the result of a fear of being criticized for making deals with foreigners is open for speculation.

Private adoption agencies like ours, as well those of some dedicated officials overseas, have made up for their lack of enthusiasm.

Here is our road map for setting up our agency's foreign adoption programs, which sounds a lot easier than it is.

A. Pre-trip activities for the agency

1. Correspond with the national welfare authorities, and if they're open to international adoption, get an appointment.

2. Contact the U.S. consulate for that country and set an appointment with them as well.

3. Use networking and government resources to find a representative to coordinate the adoptions.

B. Activities in the country we're visiting

1. Meet the authorities to obtain an approval or license.

2. Hire a representative to coordinate the adoptions and cooperate with the agency, the government welfare authorities, and the courts. (Easier said than done. Ever try supervising employees by remote control? Representatives we hire must be so self-disciplined that they don't need much supervision.)

3. Visit the orphanages to informally inspect them and determine the standard of care.

4. Take the officials out to dinner. Expect rounds of speeches in languages you don't understand. Applaud anyway. In some countries you can also expect rounds of toasts. If they're used to alcohol and you're not, tell them that you don't drink, so you can keep a sharp mind throughout the evening.

I've lost track of the number of adoption trips we've taken, but the one that stands out in my mind is an aborted flight to Guatemala that went awry at the airport in Houston. We were pressed backward at top speed and suddenly thrown forward in a full screeching stop. The overheated tires blew out. The cargo hold flew open, spewed baggage, and left it scattered along the runway.

My husband and I were among the dazed but thankful passengers ushered out of the plane without any explanation. We spent hours waiting for new tires and got to know our fellow travelers. We met a church group on a medical mission, whose desperate prayers for a safe stop were as quiet as mine. And we got to know six delightful but "illegal" Latin teenagers that an immigration officer was escorting back home. The four boys and two girls were well-groomed, energetic, and earnest; all they wanted were jobs, so they could send money home to their families. Unknown to the officer, Latin American passengers were slipping them dictionaries and the contact information of their American relatives. "Learn better English, and you won't get caught again," they were told.

When we boarded again, we were flown to El Salvador for the night. The airline put us up in a splendid hotel and treated us to a free dinner and breakfast in the restaurant. The teenagers sat at a table across from us. Their eyes bulged over the menus and the prices.

"What a country," one of the kids said to another. "I got to America on foot, and I'm being sent home in style! I'll be back." The teenagers were from Guatemala, Mexico, and El Salvador. Their nations' economies and distributions of wealth were robbing these kids of a decent future. They each had a family, but no hope for further education or even an unskilled job. What I had seen prior to these teenagers were impoverished mothers whose survival depended on relinquishing their babies. The girls and boys in this group of illegal immigrants were prime candidates for leaving a baby behind to be raised by others, relinquishing a baby to an orphanage, or abandoning it altogether.

The first trip my husband and I took to an orphanage in Latin America was overwhelming, partly because we were adopting for the first time, and partly because I had never seen children begging on the street or visited a children's institution before. Compared to the life of children on the street, the life of children in the orphanage was an improvement. But compared to life in an emotionally and financially stable family, the orphanage existence came up short.

Adoptive parents are always amazed that so few of the children in a typical orphanage are available for adoption. If one hundred children of various ages lived in the orphanage, fewer than half might be available for adoption. A lot of them have been taken away by court order from neglectful, abusive parents by welfare authorities. (In Russia, as long as a relative occasionally visits a child, officials often hold off in attempting to terminate the parental rights in court unless adoptive parents show interest in the child.) The rest of the orphanage children are considered likely to have been abandoned, and efforts are made to find their biological relatives by publishing their photos and full names (if known) in the newspaper. If no relative steps forward during an allotted time period of three to six months or some other specified time frame, the child is issued a certificate of abandonment and is available for adoption.

Children admitted to government orphanages in Eastern Europe have a vastly different experience than those sheltered in the private nonprofit agencies in Latin America. Even some of the Eastern European orphanage directors I've spoken to agree that the private Colombian adoption agencies' model is a lot better, because it simulates a family. In fact some Russian regions are already setting up family-style foster homes.

In countries south of our border, a lot of children are cared for in private, licensed, family-style dwellings. Infants and children have separate living quarters but intermingle during meals and playtimes like a real family. Infants and toddlers learn to socialize and speak by interacting with older children as well as the caregivers. In some orphanages, older children pick a baby or toddler as their special little friend. As a result, the children usually meet their developmental milestones earlier than those in the typical Eastern European orphanage.

The Bulgarian, Romanian, Russian, and Ukrainian orphanages I've visited are divided by specific age groups. This is also true of countries formerly dominated by the Soviet Union, such as Kazakhstan and Mongolia. They usually follow this pattern: Infants to three-year-olds live in "baby houses." From the age of four to six or seven, they're in an orphanage for that age group. Children over six or seven are transferred to an orphanage where they stay until the age of emancipation.

> Orphanage Discharge: Worldwide, emancipation from an orphanage is around age fourteen in some countries and age seventeen in others. Even if provisions have been made for shelter and job training, the teenagers face an uncertain future when they have no family to provide encouragement and support.

China separates children by age as well, but the majority are abandoned a day or two after birth and placed with families abroad within a year or less. On our first trip to China, we saw that each orphanage had the infants' formulas and schedules posted on a blackboard. Tiny infants wore diapers wrapped with recycled plastic bags. I thought the posted schedule sensible and the crafting of leakproof diaper covers ingenious.

In orphanages there is little opportunity for children separated into age groups to socialize with anyone outside of their peers. Two-year-olds can't learn to speak or even socialize nicely from other two-year-olds. This is the main reason so many children are delayed in speech and motor skills. At breakfast, lunch, and supper, the children are encouraged to finish their food quickly and get down from the table. No one caters to picky eaters or slowpokes. And of course, no one asks them what they would like to eat. When the majority of children at the table have finished, the food is put away and the tables and floors cleaned. Children are seldom spoken to at meals, not even those who still need to be fed by a nanny. Nannies who like children make eye contact and small talk. But others just do the job and look bored.

In the Eastern European orphanages I visited, toilet training began as soon as a child could sit on a potty. They all stayed in the same room on the potties until each had a bowel movement. This takes at least an hour; you have to wonder how the nannies make the children stay in place that long. Then the children are bathed and dressed.

Babies are held under a faucet of running water. Then, after they're able to stand up, they are thrust under a cold shower. When children first see a Western-style bathtub, they're overwhelmed. It takes a lot of smiles, bubbles, and bath toys to convince them that bath time is fun time.

None of the orphanages I toured in Bulgaria, Romania, or Russia used diapers. During the day, the toddlers were put in huge playpens or on the floor in playrooms. In the better institutions, the children were taken outside every day, which not only provides exercise but prevents the vitamin D deficiency, called rickets, that affects the bones. After lunch the children are dressed in clean clothes and put down for naps.

When I asked the directors why they didn't use diapers, they usually said something like, "We already have too much laundry to do every day. Look at these piles of dirty clothes!" The lack of diapers and waterproof pants supposedly saved on the amount of laundry. But it took its toll in sanitation. A lot of toddlers immigrate with intestinal parasites. Fortunately these are generally easy to treat, if discovered soon after the child arrives, but certain parasites, like giardia, can be hard to detect without multiple repeated tests.

Caitlin, whom I observed, had been institutionalized in a Bulgarian orphanage. She had been there since she was a week old. At eighteen months, she had reached the legal age at which she could be referred for adoption. Although she looked me in the eye, she spent most of her time with me slowly spinning around. I hoped it was an evasion technique she had developed, rather than autism. She babbled at me, and when I talked to her, she babbled even more. I had nothing else to go on, but my intuition told me this child would do well in an adoptive home.

Caitlin immigrated to the United States about six months after I met her. She was adopted by a no-nonsense couple who determinedly saw her through furious temper tantrums over every little change. Bath time was a horror for her; no amount of fragrant bubble bath could change her mind. Gradually the couple won her heart and her cooperation. Six months later, she was a well-bonded member of the family: she spoke English, got along well with everyone, and displayed a very sweet nature. She later showed herself to be an excellent student who impressed one of her teachers so much that the teacher adopted a child through our agency. Caitlin is another happy child who proves how resilient children can be.

> Institutional life slows a child's growth and hampers his or her development. All countries, and our own fifty states, need to terminate the rights of abandoning, neglectful, abusive biological parents within six months of a child's admission to foster care or an orphanage, so that the child can be adopted. Pretty little Caitlin is a child who pediatricians would call "resilient."

The Peace Palace, The Hague, Holland

1. The Erichsen family, 1984

2. The Erichsen family, 1998

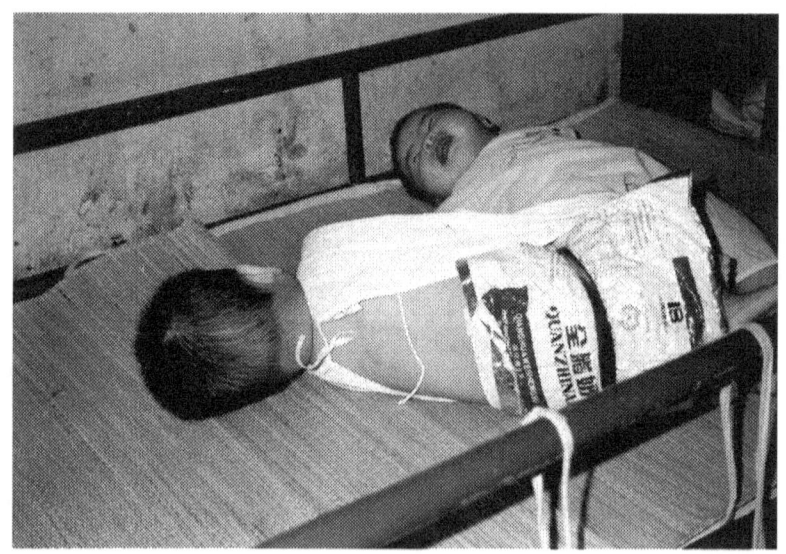

3. Asian orphanage

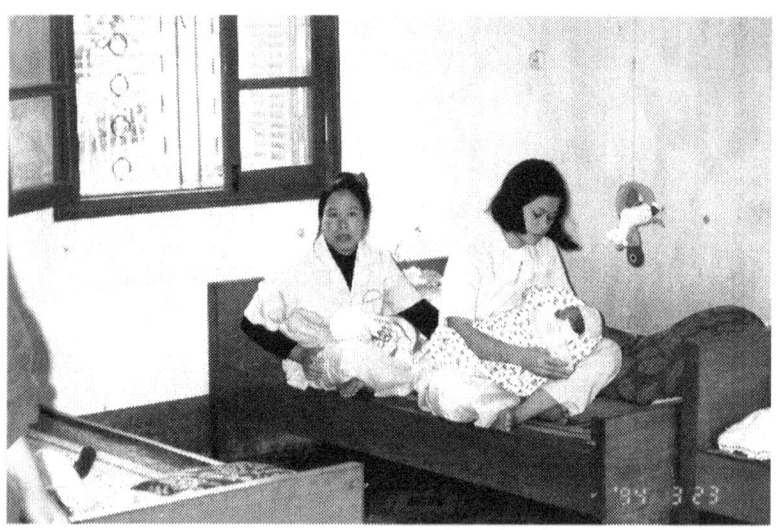

4. Asian orphanage interior with nannies

5. Diaper-less Russian Roma infant

6. Abandoned Russian children's shelter

7. Typical cement playground in orphanages

8. Jean with Caitlin in Bulgaria

9. Caitlin in the United States after adoption by David and Sara Nickel

10. Ken and Ruth Arnold with daughter Rebecca

11. Ruth and Rebecca at an LNI children's party

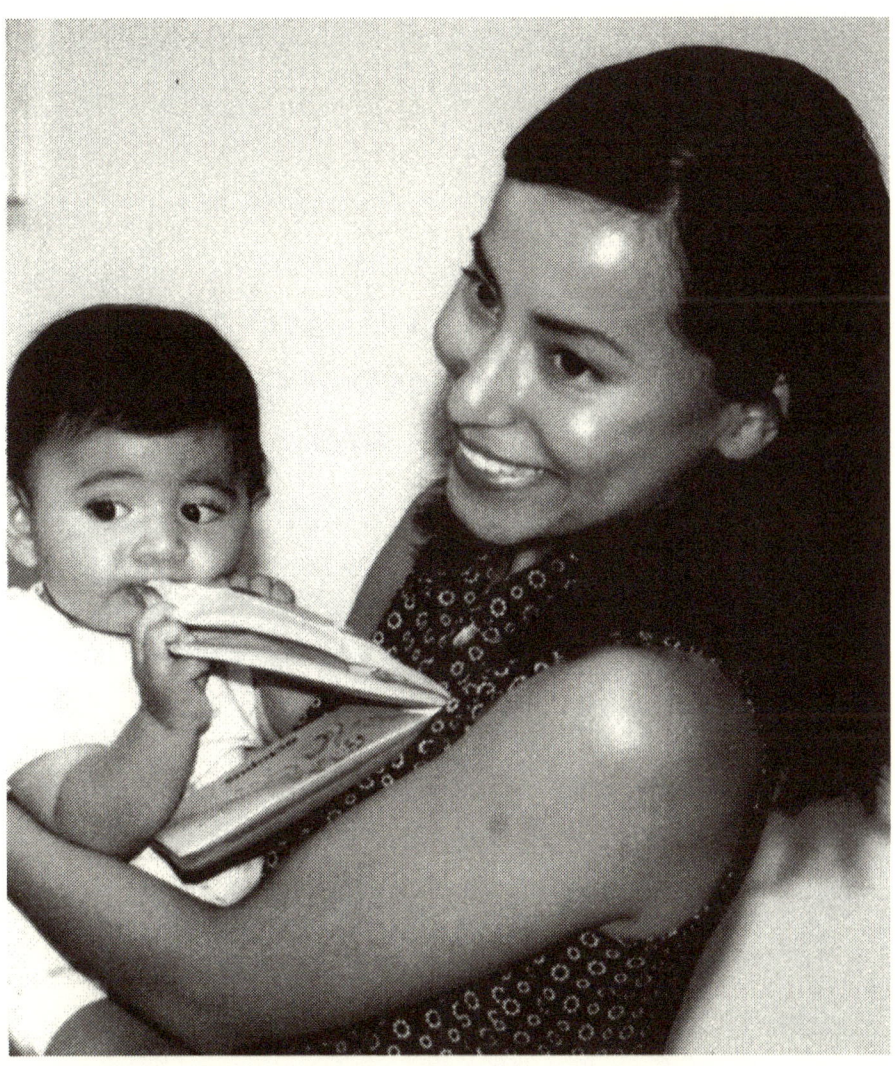

12. Rosana Erichsen, Executive Director, LNI, with Guatemalan baby

13. Sara and Darin Alley with "Best Men" Serge and Sasha

6

Hosting Foreign Adoption Authorities

Here in America, we have an immensely humorous people in a land of milk and honey and wit, who cherish the ideal of the "sense" of humor and at the same time are highly suspicious of anything that is non-serious.

—E.B. White

A funny thing happened on our way to the Eastern Hemisphere.

Other American agencies got there before we did. Experienced agencies with humanitarian concerns worked with key people to institute policies and programs to benefit homeless children. Unfortunately some of the Americans held out a golden carrot to foreign welfare staff: a two-week vacation to the United States, all expenses paid. In response the grateful foreign welfare folks, who had never traveled abroad, always produced a good-bye gift. Inevitably the gifts were impressive...and big. Heavy. Unwieldy. Highly jettisonable. Yet the awkward gifts weren't punishment enough for shortsighted agency directors whose offers produced a ripple effect that sent officials of every nationality to our doors. Didn't anyone realize that as host, the adoption agency would be responsible for the well-being, health, and safety of these guests? There wasn't insurance for this.

The rumor that American agencies were giving away free trips spread like wildfire. At our appointments with foreign welfare directors, they always brought up the subject of a free trip. When could they come? They were usually available to travel anytime except their national holidays. Such-and-such an agency had already promised to host them, but they wanted to see us as well—our state, our office—and to visit the adoptive families. Because most of them didn't speak English and had never traveled outside of their countries before, our bilingual representatives had to accompany them. Welfare staff who had never traveled outside their countries were suddenly jet-setters who saw more of the United States in five years than the typical American sees in a lifetime.

Eventually we stopped working in the countries where these excessive demands were made. But the memories linger on.

Some of the travelers with the highest expectations came from the Eastern European country of Romania. The welfare deputies had been wined and dined by Western European adoption units to the point that they were highly discriminating. Before arriving in Houston in 1998, they insisted on a luxury hotel with French-speaking staff and a daily schedule of events. I was under the mistaken impression that they wanted to know and understand the adoption process in the United States and see some of the happy families. We scheduled time at our agency office for meetings and hastened to make dates for lunch and visits to several local adoptive homes; I e-mailed the Romanians the itinerary. But when the visitors arrived, they told me (through our bilingual representative) that they had no interest in any adoption-related activities. They wanted to sightsee, and they needed a lot of days just to shop!

When I called the adoptive parents to cancel our arrangements, I discovered that our families had been honored to be chosen as hosts and were already cooking special dishes for the Romanians. They were genuinely disappointed. So was I. Our staff had to take the Romanians to the mall and watch over them. We touched base with the Romanians at the hotel several times, just to make sure they were all right. They were more than all right. They ordered the most expensive wine and gourmet meals. I waited impatiently for their departure date. Grinning smugly, I watched the Romanians trundle to the airport's departure lounge, breathing heavily, weighed down by the burden of their purchases.

Several years later, the game was up. Their cushy government positions were lost and gone forever. Romania had clamped a moratorium on international adoptions.

Just as buying too much abroad is insane, packing properly for a trip abroad is extremely important to the adoptive parent's health and comfort. Observe the tiny suitcases of international cabin attendants, and you'll understand that less is more. Over the years, I've produced lists of what to pack to cover casual and formal affairs in all kinds of weather. But the feedback I get from our representatives abroad tells me my advice is largely ignored. Adoptive families arrive exhausted, with so many bags that two cars are needed to take two people and their luggage to a hotel. If the family has to travel to distant parts and brings back one or more children, the baggage problem multiplies like the stash of a pack rat's treasure trove.

Although most of the men on our Russian staff fumed about the amount, as well as the size and weight, of our client's baggage, this excess did not make an impression on our Russian bilingual representative, Tatiana, who had attached herself to a delegation from her region in Russia. We tried to cut costs by putting the visitors up in an apartment hotel and stocking their refrigerator with Russian items so they could make some of their own meals.

Six feet tall and willowy, Tatiana looked like a model...except for her eternally glum expression. She struggled under the load of two huge, old-fashioned leather suitcases when she deplaned. She accompanied women who officiated over the welfare of orphans in their regions. Their arrival coincided with our annual international family celebration. Families who had adopted from Russia, as well as from Asian and Latin American countries, attended this event. The Russian women mingled with our transracial families. One of them, who was from a region with Asian and indigenous populations, was impressed to see that white people could love nonwhite children as their own. Through Tatiana, she said, "I'm taking pictures back with me. Russians won't believe this. They still think that if they have to adopt, it's a disgrace. They want white children, so that they don't have to explain anything." Her colleagues expressed similar views.

In the olden days, we had found welfare officials, attorneys, and LNI representatives via the U.S. consulate's network and international contacts, in all of the countries where we had programs. Nowadays foreign entrepreneurs contact us by e-mail, along with dozens of other agencies they find on the Internet. In either case, we must screen carefully for trustworthy, dependable representatives and welfare officials. But there's no way to figure out how well they travel.

PART III
Practical Considerations

7

Identifying Adoptable Children

Somehow destiny comes into play. These children end up with you,
and you end up with them. It's something quite magical.

—Nicole Kidman, adoptive parent

Children are adopted by nonresidents in nearly every developing nation, with
the exception of most Islamic countries. According to the U.S. State Department,
4,017 children, mainly Asian, were immigrated by U.S. citizens in 1973. At that
time, my husband and I adopted in Colombia and had made inroads as research-
ers to the rest of Latin America. Other agencies and facilitators followed suit. By
1990 South Korea, Colombia, Peru, and the Philippines placed the most children. Then, after the Soviet Union fell apart in 1991, Bulgaria, Romania, Russia,
and Ukraine opened their doors to international adoption. China opened in
1992, closed in 1993, and reopened in 1994.

At that point, international adoptions increased exponentially. According to
an article in *U.S. News & World Report* dated June 6, 2005, "From 1990 to 2004,
the list of countries allowing the most foreign adoptions changed dramatically.
By 2005, 22,728 children, mainly from China, Guatemala, and Russia, were
adopted by citizens of the United States." Colombia, where we had put a lot of
effort, placed 631 children in 1990. After that the Colombian government made
quite a few legislative changes. In 2004 only 287 children were adopted by U.S.
citizens. For a complete breakdown of the worldwide statistics, visit
travel.state.gov.

Although the United States receives the most children from abroad, Western
European nations adopt a lot of children too. As in the United States, few chil-
dren are available for adoption in developed Western European countries such as
Denmark, Germany, Italy, Norway, Spain, Sweden, and the Netherlands. A

whole generation of children from undeveloped countries in Asia, Eastern Europe, and Africa have grown up with adoptive families in Western Europe.

Immigration laws in those countries are less stringent than ours, but the wait for a child can be twice as long. Home studies are conducted by government officials, and there may be an internal waiting list within the country before the family can submit an application abroad. U.S. citizens have rigid requirements to follow: in order to bring children into the United States, an orphan petition must be filed with the Citizenship and Immigration Service (CIS) of the United States, which in turn obtains an FBI clearance of the prospective adoptive parents before granting its approval with a form called an I-171H. The FBI's search of fingerprint records safeguards children from known criminals.

CIS is a gatekeeper. The service demands a home study as well as identifying documentation such as health and social information on the prospective parents and the child. CIS forms I-600A and I-600 explain the documentation required for a child to emigrate. In almost every case, the children are homeless due to poverty or social pressure. A legal certificate of abandonment or death certificates for the parents, or a documented termination of parental rights, is required for a child to be considered adoptable. Institutionalized children from two-parent, impoverished families qualify, provided that both parents sign the relinquishment forms. But children placed directly by a relative can have only one living legal parent, with documentation proving that this parent is incapable of providing support.

Along with these mandatory documents, a written and translated evaluation of the child's health and social background is required. This is prepared in the child's homeland and ranges from a complete medical report, as in China, to one that is nearly unintelligible to Westerners, as in Russia. Prospective parents must gauge the physical and emotional health and development of a child in strange surroundings—usually in an unknown language with unfamiliar medical terms. Every adoptive parent faces a decisive moment. They can't count on the cursory physical by a U.S. embassy-approved physician. Few children are denied entry by the United States, except those with psychiatric disorders, severe mental retardation, and dangerous contagious diseases.

- **Tip**: Learn how to look for signs and symptoms of common diseases found in institutionalized children. Study the medical section of *How to Adopt Internationally*.

This is the time to arrange for a preadoption consultation at an international pediatric clinic. They can be found in nearly every state. A list of such clinics is available on the Internet. The clinics will provide you with excellent advice and developmental checklists and will be available for phone or e-mail consultations while you're abroad. Although you will receive a social history on the mother (if known) and the child, and a health report with updates only an experienced health professional can evaluate the information and the photos you e-mail them in order to provide an assessment.

In the future, child referrals should feel less worrisome to prospective adopters, because adoption agencies will be required to provide more information and support. The Hague Convention mandates that adoption agencies provide adoptive parents with a training session of two hours to help prepare them for the adoption of a particular child. Preceding this, an additional eight hours of training must cover the child's cultural, racial, religious, ethnic, and linguistic background, as well as his or her medical and social history.

There is one category of children that is denied entry: refugee children. Although adoption agencies are swamped with calls from folks who want to adopt after every war and natural disaster, the children left homeless are not immediately placed in adoptive homes. They remain in refugee camps until every attempt to find relatives has failed. It takes years to clarify the status of such children.

The tragic lesson the world learned toward the end of the war in Vietnam now keeps refugee children in limbo. Hundreds of children came from South Vietnam via Operation Babylift, where, in order to save their lives, they were carried to American military planes by their parents, who thought they would never see them again.

Adoption agencies in the United States placed the children in adoptive homes. The children were jolted into a King Solomon situation several years after the operation. A lot of the children's parents survived and immigrated to the United States. They immediately sought help in locating their children. Because these parents had never signed legal relinquishment forms, their parental rights were never terminated. It sometimes took a court order to remove the children from their heartbroken American parents and reunite them with biological parents they barely remembered. The courts still believe that blood is thicker than water.

8

Traveling Abroad to Adopt, Emigrate, and Immigrate a Child

What a curious thing is adoption. We have been the legal parents of Masha for less than a week, but I feel profoundly that she is my own. Whatever the doctor had said, my only concern was how to cope—never the thought of returning her.

—Ruth Arnold, adoptive mother

In an ideal world, adoption would be turned upside down to make children the clients. They're a lot more in need of hand-holding, emotional support, and medical attention than the adults who adopt them. But until orphanages are replaced by licensed, supervised foster homes abroad, children won't get this kind of attention.

Once your agency and the other entities involved approve you, your names are added to a waiting pool, along with the age and gender of the child you desire from a particular country.

Waiting is the most difficult part for potential parents. Most social workers would refer a baby to prospective parents within nine months after they finish their documentation and parent-training courses if they could. Psychologically it makes sense. Prospective adoptive parents wait for referral information with a schedule in mind, just as they would await the birth of a child. Unfortunately, unseen legal and political barriers can prevent this from happening within the estimated time frame. But sooner or later, referral information will come your way that hopefully is accurate.

Ruth Arnold describes her reactions to her child's records:

> As I read the one page of sketchy information, my heart sank. Alcoholic parents, premature birth, institutionalized from one month of age, developmen-

tally slow—and what was most worrisome of all, her head measurement was too small, a possible indicator of fetal alcohol syndrome.

The video offered no real encouragement. Masha, our prospective daughter, rubbed her eyes, poked at her neck, walked briefly across the screen, and uttered one word, "kukla" (doll). What's more, there was clearly a problem with her eyes: they didn't focus together. And the medical report—which made free use of words like hypostasis and hypotrophy (of the second degree, yet) made no mention of her eyes. Could this be the daughter of our dreams? Frankly it didn't seem likely.

The only hopeful information was a description of Masha's current accomplishments—she walks, she talks in full sentences, she knows her colors, she can differentiate large from small.

Our pediatrician agreed to review all the materials, so I rushed the package to him. I spent the weekend on the phone talking to other parents who had adopted from the same region. They all agreed that the developmental information they received at placement was much more accurate than the medical. While I agonized over the decision, our pediatrician called. He did more than give me the go-ahead—he was positively enthusiastic.

"Her head's fine," he said. "She looks great. Take her."

So Monday morning, I called and accepted the placement. Did I feel exhilarated that we'd finally found our daughter? No, I was terrified. What about fetal alcohol syndrome, emotional attachment disorder, or mental disabilities? From then until I actually held Masha in my arms (at which point all my worries miraculously dissipated), worry was my constant companion.

Once we were back in the States with Masha in tow, our pediatrician told me she was healthy. He measured her head and said it was small but in proportion to her other measurements. I, frankly, see no signs of mental slowness. Masha only needs to be shown something once, and then she remembers. She is bright, curious, and lots of fun. I can't believe I spent sleepless nights worrying over accepting this placement.

Most people need emotional support during the delay between the referral, a possible visit in the child's country, and the adoption. It's a good time for you to call recently returned adoptive parents for backup. A description of their child's physical condition and behavior will help you get ready for what may await you. The younger the child, the less likely you will have behavioral problems at the outset, but you can still expect some degree of malnutrition and developmental delays. These can generally be fixed. As for the behavior, child psychologists say there are three groups of children: about 20 percent are called the "resilient rascals," because they come here and thrive right away; about 60 percent are called "wounded warriors," because they have serious problems but get better after the first year or so; and another 20 percent are called "challenged children" and may require lifelong help.

Jayne Gordon had some initial concerns about her Asian child:

> Willow became my daughter in November 1999. I will always cherish the moment she was placed in my arms. She was so tiny! She weighed sixteen pounds and looked to be about seven months old, even though she was about fourteen months old. I had heard that the orphanages weren't heated, but I wasn't prepared for the fact that she had eight layers of clothes on that prevented her from using her arms and legs. When I took her back to my hotel and peeled off most of her layers, I discovered that Willow was unable to maintain a sitting position, and her arms and legs were floppy and useless. But she caught on! She began crawling in late February 2000, walking in May 2000, and talking in May 2000. Willow likes to giggle and to give hugs and kisses. She also likes to run and climb and talks in two-word phrases like her two-year-old friends. Willow has brought joy in my life, and I thank God for her. I also pray for her biological mother to be comforted, for I know that giving her up was a heartbreaking decision.

Willow's placement was typically abrupt; such an approach is common in most countries. The child is usually plunked into the adoptive parents' arms soon after their arrival. The Hague Convention does not address this issue, yet experts agree that the transition to a new family should instead be a gradual one. Your strange look, smell, and speech may cast fear in the heart of the little one you've come so far to adopt. Depending on the child's age, temperament, and the circumstances surrounding the initial placement, it can take days, weeks, months, or years for secure bonding and attachment between the parents and the child to occur. Quick, efficient placements—without regard for the child's emotional needs—are the norm in international adoptions. They are usually geared toward time constraints of the adoption authorities or the adoptive parents instead of the child's need for stability.

- **Tip:** Adoptive parents can do a lot to make their first contact with the child successful. Approach the child slowly and quietly. Speak in a low voice. Wear clothing that is soft in texture and muted in color. Avoid eye contact until the child looks at you.

Few countries require a bonding period of several weeks, as most of our states do. In Brazil, Kazakhstan, and Russia, placements are usually scheduled with visits over several weeks. Ideally you visit the child for successively longer periods of time before you take the child to your home (in some cases, your hotel or apartment) to visit you. Again, the visits are gradually lengthened until the child stays overnight and returns to the foster home or orphanage for a last visit before you take physical custody. Even then the child may have never ridden in a car or have been inside a building other than the orphanage; the child may get carsick. And just when the children are getting accustomed to the changes, they're carried onto an airplane and expected to sit still and not cry during the long flight to their new home. Adoptive parents should stay abroad longer than most countries require, so that the transition can be carefully planned with the child's emotional needs in mind.

Occasionally the adoption is disrupted by the adoptive parents after a sudden, traumatic placement because of their inability to cope with the child's initial reactions of fear, withdrawal, anger, or inconsolable crying. A child's intense reactions can last for several days or more.

Most adoptive parents are mature enough to understand what the child is going through. With the assistance of their agency's representative, they joyfully follow the rules and regulations. The child emigrates by leaving his or her homeland and immigrates by entering the United States as a permanent resident on an IR-3 or IR-4 visa.

The child's immigration is usually more traumatic and the parents' adjustment more difficult when he or she is adopted by proxy and brought to the United States by a stranger (escorted), or adopted and brought to the United States by only one spouse on an IR-4 visa. The Hague Convention has specific post-placement requirements for this type of adoption, which must be conducted by a social worker. When these visits are concluded, the new parents must readopt the child and apply for U.S. citizenship. The child is considered an alien by CIS until U.S. citizenship is granted. By contrast, when both parents visit the child prior to adopting her or him abroad, the Hague Convention deems this post-adoption. The child is immigrated on an IR-3 visa. Any visitation requirements by a social worker are solely those of the child's country of origin. A certificate of citizenship is automatically sent to the child approximately forty-five days after immigration.

The majority of adoptive parents are highly responsible and follow the post-adoption or post-placement procedures and rules laid down by their county court and CIS. Unfortunately I've heard of cases where procrastinating or uninformed parents ignored these steps. Over the course of my social work practice, folks have called who weren't even our clients but saw me as the last resort. For example, a stressed-out mom, Linda (not her real name), called me in a fury on the first day of public school. The child whom Linda had adopted as a baby five years before and renamed Jessica (not her real name), had been denied admittance.

When the school had asked for identification, Linda showed them Jessica's passport. The names didn't match. Jessica's legal name was still the one she was given in China. Linda sputtered that she had not reaffirmed the foreign decree in her county court and officially changed Jessica's name, because she hadn't wanted to deal with any more paperwork. Linda was angry when I told her there was no way out of it, and Jessica was upset that she might miss several months of school on account of it.

Further examples show how parents who don't apply for a child's U.S. citizenship can put children in a financial bind or in danger of deportation. The worried mother of an eighteen-year-old Latina called for guidance, because she couldn't get government loans for her college-bound daughter. The panicked mother of a teenage boy caught stealing begged me for assistance, because he was in danger of being deported to Central America—a place he barely remembered.

On separate occasions, I heard from two men born and adopted in South America who are now in their thirties. Both were in the midst of a crisis. The first called because he had lost his job and couldn't get hired anywhere else, and the other, around the same age, couldn't leave the United States with his military unit, all because of their alien status. Their green cards were no longer valid. Problems like this continue to happen. Agencies must follow up routinely with their families to make certain that the children qualify for public school, along with state and federal programs, and will not become stateless persons in danger of deportation. Social workers must take time with new parents to stress the importance of officially changing the child's name if necessary, readopting or reaffirming the foreign adoption decree, and applying for U.S. citizenship.

When a child first immigrates, a close follow-up by the social worker helps parents understand the underlying needs of the child. This way, if the child has health or behavioral problems or developmental delays, the social worker will help find resources to identify them and refer the family to the appropriate professionals. The longer the treatment is put off, the longer it usually takes to treat the problem.

Regardless of the child's background or problems, the privacy of the family should be respected after legal adoption. Twelve to twenty-four months after the adoption seems long enough to most families. On the one hand, parents should feel free to choose whether they want to maintain a relationship with the agency and the foreign country beyond this time. They believe they should be granted some kind of sovereignty. They should feel entitled to raise the child. Eighteen years of annual reports required by a few countries feels like an imposition to a lot of folks. On the other hand, countries that have read media reports of child abuse by American adoptive families are understandably concerned and anxious to see parents' or agencies' annual reports, and the glowing letters and heartwarming photographs are very reassuring to them.

Registration at the consulate is another sticking point for some parents. Some Eastern European countries require that the adopted child's new name and address be registered at their consulate in the United States. This mandate strikes fear in the hearts of some adoptive parents, who worry that a consular official will pay a visit and shake the child's trust in their permanence with the family. However, this worry is probably not realistic.

Once a family is home and the parents have had time to reflect, they realize that timing was everything. They look back at the circumstances that led them, at that particular time, to that particular child, in that particular country, and are filled with wonder—the child is perfect for them! This feeling is unique in the realm of human experience.

After parenting children for half a century and observing families as a social worker for half that long, I know what it takes to raise a child who is rapidly growing and developing. While we do this job, we are not even done with our own maturation and emotional development. I once asked myself whether the high praise afforded most parents in home studies is really true. Are we as flexible, tolerant, and patient as we thought?

Sara Graham proved that she had those qualities when a translator made an incredible mistake on the referral documents. She wrote:

> In September 1997, I returned from Russia after adopting Alexander and Sergei, who were four years old at the time. The only surprise I got was that we had *thought* I was adopting Sergei and Alexandra. It was quite a (pleasant) shock to find that I had two wonderful (identical!) boys instead of a boy and a girl. But things worked out perfectly. I could not ask for more wonderful children.
>
> Here is an update. The boys are doing fantastic. They will be nine years old in June. They are both honor students at school, and they are a joy both at home and (I'm told) at school.
>
> There has also been a very exciting development in all of our lives. "We" got married in June. I use the term "we" because that is how the boys refer to it. The boys were best men at our wedding. They now have a great dad. He officially adopted the boys six months later. They are so happy, and they, in turn, enrich our lives beyond belief.

9

A Day Inside the Agency

Always remember the Golden Rule:
Do unto others what you would have them do unto you.

On a typical day, the agency staff is busily communicating with eager prospective parents and our representatives abroad to clarify the paperwork, obtain updated information, or address possible concerns. Each day is not a crisis. But when one occurs, it's memorable.

May 1, 1984: A cockeyed sight greeted me as I stepped inside the agency. Carmen (not her real name), our refined, well-groomed receptionist, looked up and said, "Gu-u-u-ud mohning," as she always did. This time, though, she had unknowingly rubbed off her carefully penciled-in left eyebrow. Poised with ramrod stringency over the phone, she was accepting calls and directing them with steely politeness. I could tell she was regally annoyed. Someone had insulted her, and it was my job to figure out who before she got up and quit.

Carmen was our first employee in a chain of skilled and reliable Mexican Americans that we hired in Austin, Texas, but she was the only one born in Mexico who had grown up in an orphanage. She had waited an entire childhood for her parents to return. Finally the nuns had given up and had arranged an early marriage for her. She told me her husband had been a lot older, had owned a successful business, and had been extremely controlling of her. In Mexico they had lived in a beautiful home. They had two children together. Carmen had finally gotten the family she had always longed for, but by the time we met her fifteen years later, she had become a widow with children to support with no outside assistance. Her mother-in-law had never accepted her because of her orphaned status and had made sure Carmen ended up with nothing. Carmen told me her family now lived in her brother's garage. She was tiny but strong, a realistic woman who never gave up.

I leaned over and said, "What's going on?"

"Meesus Erichsen, zee phone ees driving me bananas. Everyone has heard about zee trouble in Honduras, and each one has already called to see if zee story ees true." She rolled her eyes. "When I came to work, another fax was waiting from Mona Scott (not her real name), but zees was ten pages long, written in longhand and covering every detail since the day she applied here. She wants to know, for zee tenth time, why she can't go back to Honduras to pick up her son this week. She insists that Heino call her zee minute he arrives in the office."

I looked at Carmen again. Her patience was wearing thin with the clients, and theirs with us. She, who had endured so much, couldn't understand why these families couldn't cope with uncertainty. However, I understood the prospective parents' angst. The prospective parents had waited far too long for the children they had visited many months previously. And Mona had waited longer than anyone.

Carmen continued, "When Meester Erichsen came in and saw the fax, eet was…like waving zee red flag…in front of zee bull! He grabbed eet out of my hand and stomped to his office." We both knew what had happened next: he bravely dialed her number. Mona's passive-aggressive behavior toward our staff was legendary. Once she said hello, a pregnant silence followed. The caller was always left dangling on the defensive, babbling feebly.

There was really nothing new to tell Mona. When the courts decided to finalize the adoption, they would do so. They controlled the fate of the children and their adoptions. If the First Lady, the titular head of national child welfare, took an extended European vacation, the children would have to wait until she returned to sign off on the adoption decree. Over the years, this pattern repeated itself in much of the rest of Latin America and Eastern Europe: a judge, a prosecutor, or officials within a national child-welfare bureau could hold up an adoption indefinitely while they wrangled with us over a sudden need to update documents, as well as consular stamps and even the placement of staples. We never had any control over adoption abroad, and made this clear in our literature, but prospective parents didn't seem to hear it.

I got up the nerve to tell Carmen about her eyebrow. As I watched her carefully restore it, I asked, "What was the worst thing that happened this morning?"

She said, "Eet was another prospective parent waiting for a child from Honduras. 'You couldn't possibly understand what we're going through,' he told me."

One month later, the First Lady finally returned, and the Honduran adoption system, the Instituto Hondureño del Niño y la Familia IHNFA, completed its umpteenth scrutiny for her benefit. An IHNFA clerk called us to invite Mona to a ceremony in the capital city. The First Lady and her designated officials would sign off on the final adoption decree and place little Juan in Mona's arms. The child would be a year old by then—nine months older than when Mona first visited him. As a social worker, I worried over the family's adjustment. I fussed over the fact that the child could experience long-term feelings of insecurity. He would have every reason to be terrified of a new parent, a new environment, a new language, and a new diet. Mona was a first-time parent. Instead of adopting the smiling five-month-old she had expected, Mona would become the instant mother of a frightened one-year-old. Would Mona be up to the reality of parenting such a child? Fortunately she was.

This pattern repeated itself as adoptive parents traveled abroad to adopt children that bureaucracies had kept in limbo for months and even years. Our agonizing relationship with Mona had already extended over a year and a half. Our written social evaluation of Mona and her husband, Frank (not his real name), along with U.S. immigration clearance and the preparation of documents for the court abroad, had taken four months. Then the couple had waited five months for the referral of a child. Traditionally girls are preferred by the majority of adopters, but this couple had wanted a boy. The couple was overjoyed with the photos and the child's social and medical history. They flew to visit him at a foster home and signed documents to initiate the adoption. Then they had to tear themselves away from him and go home.

The court was supposed to take five to six months to complete the adoption so that Mona and Frank could emigrate the baby. But nine months passed while they waited for finalization of the adoption. The extra three months wore them out emotionally.

When Frank and Mona returned with Juan, post-adoption visits by a social worker would follow once a month for six months. After that the family would need to send us annual reports on the child's health and development for eighteen years. These would be translated into Spanish and sent to IHNFA. I worried that Mona wouldn't cooperate. Instead she was cooperative—but voluble, and needed to vent. A call from our licensing consultant clinched it: Mona had formally complained, and they would be coming out to investigate.

Strong coffee was called for on that fateful day. My hands were shaking as I measured the coffee grinds and water, poured them into the coffeemaker, and plugged it in. I had no idea what an investigation would entail. The gurgling sounds of the coffeemaker were reassuring.

Our licensing consultant saw what we were up against. According to the consultant, what had seemed instinctive to me needed to be reiterated in a contract:

"The child is not your child until you hold the adoption decree, arrive at a port of entry in the United States, submit the child's documents and U.S. orphan visa to an immigration official, and the child is granted permission to immigrate."

- **Tip:** Don't be lulled into believing that your approval of a child's referral makes him or her yours. Think with your head, not your heart, during the long process of adopting abroad.

Honduras—and every other country, for that matter—is responsible for children born within its borders. It is the country, not our agency, that controls the fate of the children and the adoption process. This wording, translated into legalese, was included in the clients' contracts after that. Not that it helped much. Prospective parents bond with a child's picture and are usually unable to relax and let legal matters run their course. They may say to an agency director, "We paid you a lot of money. Why don't you put some pressure on them?" But the phrase I hate most from prospective adopters is, "What can I do to make this happen?" I'm always afraid they're talking about bribes.

My answer is, "Keep on top of your documents and U.S. Citizenship and Immigration Service forms. You need up-to-date approvals and clearances when the court is ready to issue the adoption decree."

"Yeah, I know," is the usual deflated response.

As I went over Frank and Mona's file with the licensing consultant, we read the approved social evaluation conducted by a certified social worker. She recommended them for the adoption of a child under one year. We reviewed the psychological evaluation, medical statements, and references. They were physically healthy and mentally stable. They didn't have any addictions. We scanned their letters of employment. We looked over their FBI fingerprint cards. They had no record, not even a misdemeanor or a driving infringement. Profiles of Mona and her husband emerged: They were of average height, weight, and possessed a quiet demeanor. Husband: computer programmer. Wife: office manager. The social worker noted that both of them were highly organized at work and at home. The licensing consultant could find nothing wrong with them and nothing wrong with our agency. The couple was obviously intolerant of what they viewed as a slipshod process with inexplicable delays. "I'm going to tell them this is not a licensing issue," she said. The staff and I breathed a sigh of relief.

This unnerving pattern repeated itself over the years, thanks to the languorous attitudes of foreign judges or unscrupulous baby brokers in several countries. In these countries, a formulaic event sequence evolved: referral, delays, adoption, waiting period; or adoption, scandal, temporary or permanent moratorium. The result: heartbroken prospective parents and stressed-out adoption-agency staff.

Although we were the first agency licensed in Honduras, we had already stopped taking applications for that country. When we opened a program there, we had no idea of the turmoil that would ensue. Following closely on our heels, bona fide agencies, as well as unlicensed facilitators, followed us to set up adoption programs with lawyers and con artists alike. Populated mainly by a Spanish/Indian ethnic group, Honduras was soon inundated with hundreds of white, middle-class Americans colonizing their capital city for monthlong stays with Spanish/Indian babies in tow. We sent around one hundred families there before international adoption ground to a halt.

While liberals in Honduras praised the opportunity granted to orphans who would probably never have been loved or educated in orphanages, their opponents mistrusted the motives of adoptive parents. Why would white Americans adopt brown babies? Who was benefiting the most from these adoptions? Newspaper articles appeared condemning the practice. They mentioned collusion, coercion, and baby selling. Some of the stories were true.

To ameliorate the criticism, the courts changed their procedures to allow more time to investigate the birth mother's situation and the legality of her relinquishment. They investigated the adoptive parents too. A social worker conducted a Honduran social evaluation when the couple arrived, and a psychologist tested them. Our adoptive parents were apprehensive, but they repeatedly came through with flying colors. If this was what it took to help the Hondurans accept international adoption, so be it.

That was before the presidential election. Suddenly the adoption issue evolved into a political soccer ball. To seal off the opposition, a rumor was born at a party for consular officials…a rumor so despicable that it gained momentum, spreading across Latin America and later to Europe. Twenty years later, the rumor was seized by adoption opponents in the Russian *Duma*. The story was so absurd that anyone with a modicum of sense would realize the fallacy of the baby-parts scandal: "Americans are adopting babies to sell them for organ transplants." The U.S. State Department issued a statement on this myth: usinfo.state.gov/media/Archive_Index/The_Baby_Parts_Myth.html.

The accuser neither knew of nor cared about the thorough social evaluation and criminal check adoptive parents receive before they can adopt. The rumor hit the news with devastating effects. The birth mothers who had already relinquished their babies were no longer at peace with their decision. Some American couples in Honduras had no choice but to give the babies placed with them back to the crying birth mothers. Articles and newscasts alerted the American public to the rumor, which spread faster than a kudzu vine. When it reached the eyes and ears of our clients, Carmen's expression said it best: "They went bananas." Heino and I, along with the rest of our staff, had been doing our best to calm everyone's fears of a shutdown of adoption for several months. The ugly rumor blasted our efforts into shambles. The clients had reason to worry; the last client we served waited a year for her daughter and got her out of the country just as Honduras cancelled further adoptions. Now only a handful of children are adopted each year, and those are usually placed with Honduran/American relatives in the United States.

10

Predicting the Future of
International Adoption

Growing up in a nest of foster children plunged me at an extremely early age into some of the more tragic situations that confront helpless people. And that awareness which never leaves a person and colors all that he or she does in later life can be of enormous value…It influenced all I would write.

—James A. Michener, adopted child

The numbers of children adopted internationally each year have peaked. There's a strong movement afoot, both here and abroad, to keep children in their home countries and encourage their adoptions or foster care by nationals.

Anti-international adoption forces have been around for decades. Shortly after we started helping families adopt in Colombia, the acclaimed Colombian novelist Gabriel Garcia Marquez was quoted in the July 18, 1974, article in the newspaper, *Times of the Americas*, "Americans are importing Colombian babies like bags of coffee." He went on to explain that New Yorkers were adopting in Colombia to collect more welfare benefits in the United States. No one has a wilder imagination than Garcia Marquez. Yet his remarks made great copy, and news services lapped it up.

His assessment of the situation fueled the fire of suspicion that culminated in the baby-parts scandal in Honduras. By 1992, as Latin American sources were drying up, the Iron Curtain collapsed, and we suddenly had access to Eastern European orphanages. The demand for white children far surpasses that for children of color; the majority of adoptive parents are white, and most of them want a child that looks like them. Russia was soon the country of choice, and just when the adoptions were increasing, the baby-parts rumor popped up there.

UNICEF is perhaps the largest organization to discourage international adoption. Support of the orphans in their home countries is preferred. A lot of officials abroad are also opposed, particularly the current minority of legislators in the Russian *Duma* (Congress). As a result, the number of children adopted abroad is dwindling. In 2006, U.S. citizens adopted 3,706 Russian children—a significant drop from the 5,865 children adopted in 2004. And in China, 6,493 children were adopted, a drop from 7,004 in 2004.

China recognizes its problem of abandoned children and has developed a safe, predictable adoption process that only requires two weeks of travel. You don't see street children in China. The Russian approach is very different. Most adoptable children have been relinquished by their birth parents or taken from them due to neglect and abuse. When children are institutionalized, their relatives have rights and must be contacted prior to an adoption by nonrelatives. Even so, the process is lengthy and complicated. A documentary broadcast by PBS in 2005 cited two hundred thousand institutionalized Russian children and a hundred thousand street children, with many joining their ranks or being abandoned in hospitals every day. A lot of street children die of malnutrition and drug abuse…and in winter, exposure.

Yet anti-adoption officials in the Russian *Duma* stress these facts instead: By 2005 nearly every major American newspaper had printed articles regarding the allegation that thirteen Russian children had been murdered by their American adoptive parents. There was also extensive media coverage of a high-profile case of a twelve-year-old girl rescued from her American adoptive father from a life of posing for Internet porn. Her single adoptive father had stayed one step ahead of the law until he displayed his daughter in a Disney World hotel room. A sharp-eyed vigilante finally helped bring him to justice, and the child was placed in foster care. This case happened three years prior to the last child's death, but was included in the story as if it had just happened. These newspaper stories made headlines again in Russia. Reporters lust for this type of story: ABC's *Primetime* presented a program on the murder and human trafficking of Russian orphans on December 1, 2005.

Most of these hapless children were adopted independently rather than through an accredited agency, yet the onus is on all of the agencies to prove that our prospective parents were carefully screened and vetted prior to our approval and afterward.

Picture my shock on Sunday, June 5, 2005, when my friend Cassandra Jones, media producer, called to tell me that the Associated Press had named our agency in an article titled, "Three American Agencies Lose Russia Licenses." The article went on to say that we had failed to monitor the children's well-being in their adoptive families.

Monitoring is done by visiting and interviewing the adoptive parents, then writing reports and sending them, with photos of the family, in a prescribed sequence for three years. Our representative in Russia was supposed to get the reports translated and sent to the appropriate region. Our social workers had followed up with the families, but their reports never got to their destination on time, thanks to delays all the way down the line. Previously twenty other American agencies had been cited for late post-placement reports (and for placing children when their accreditation had expired), but most were reaccredited nonetheless. For some unfathomable reason, we had been singled out for delayed reports alone.

We had been accredited three times; our last certification had run out in December 2004. The Russian accreditation process had been disrupted due to an overhaul of the government by Russia's President Putin. We had applied, then waited, along with a lot of other adoption agencies. The shocking AP article circulated quickly and kept our agency on pins and needles. When a friend with connections in the media followed up on our behalf, she communicated with a journalist based in Europe who wrote for wire services. She e-mailed us to say that the information for the article was planted by someone high up in the Russian government.

Strangely, we didn't hear directly from the authorities for months. Adoptive parents who had already visited their children were waiting for a final adoption decree, so they could return to emigrate their children. How were we to finish those cases? Where and to whom were we supposed to send the rest of the post-adoption reports that would be generated for the next three years? After twelve years working in Russia, contributing to the orphanages, and leading educational efforts, we were out in the cold. The agencies that were accredited hung on by their fingernails, never knowing when the hammer might fall. Less than a year later, the mallet struck again. Reaccreditation was denied to a lot of agencies when their accreditations expired. Instead, a precondition to apply for reaccreditation was instituted that required all foreign nonprofit organizations to be registered as a non-governmental organization (NGO) with the Ministry of Justice. By January 2007, 55 agencies had received NGO status.

A press release from the Russian Federation Education and Science Ministry, Regulations of November 4th 2006, No. 654, titled, *On Activities of the Foreign Adoption Organs [sic] and Organizations in the Russian Federation and on Control*

Over Adoption Activities, set forth the proposed resolutions that will create a new process of accreditation for agencies. Only time will tell when the regulations will go into effect and how they will be implemented.

We, along with all of the other agencies, had already lost Romania. In 2002 demands were made that Romania clean up a corrupt child-welfare system as a condition for admission to the European Union. Romanian politicians jumped into action. They passed Law 272, to halt decades of mismanagement in just a few years, with edicts that many critics now say were overzealous and impractical. The new law favored reuniting children with biological relatives or placing them in foster care. A *New York Times* article titled "New Law Leaves Romanian Orphans Stranded" quoted Gabi Mihaela Comanescu as follows: "The law says every abandoned child under two should be in foster care, but as far as I know, there aren't nearly enough foster homes." Close to ten thousand children are abandoned at hospitals each year in Romania, according to a new study by UNICEF, and up to fifty thousand children are left in the care of the state. Adoption in Bulgaria, where thousands of normal infants and children have been institutionalized by their poverty-stricken parents, slowed to a halt for the same reasons.

Los Niños International Adoption Center came full circle. After twenty-five years of placing children, first from Latin America, then Asia and Eastern Europe, we went back to where we started, but in countries with diminishing numbers of available children. Colombia is one of the few countries with licensed, nonprofit adoption agencies that shelter children. This has made it possible for the children to receive better care while they wait, and for nonresidents to better communicate and coordinate with the agencies in order to adopt. Today the wait for the referral of a Colombian infant by U.S. citizens is around two to three years, rather than a few months. Requirements for parents are extremely stringent. And the Colombian adoption committees who review couples' dossiers have no compunction about turning down couples who do not fit the requirements exactly, no matter who the couples know in high places.

Guatemala placed 4,135 children in 2006, causing raised eyebrows when compared to much lower numbers in other areas—less than fifty from neighboring El Salvador and 70 from Mexico. Guatemala is the most expensive country in the world from which to adopt. The children are relinquished by their birth mothers to lawyers in supervised settings and placed in private foster care. The adoption process drags on for about six months, and the attorneys charge fees for the legal work and private foster care services. Resolutions on declaring a moratorium on international adoption have been brought up for a vote three times in the Guatemalan Congress. The resolution was voted down the first time around. The second round was under way just before this was written and was voted down again.

A significant issue in the future of Guatemala is whether its government will conform to the mandates of the Hague Convention, which it has signed. It is possible that once the treaty takes effect, the U.S. Department of State will no longer be able to approve adoptions from that country if Guatemala has not yet changed its laws so that they are consistent with Hague regulations. Many people who favor the continuation of Guatemalan adoptions, including the Department of State and a group of Guatemalan attorneys, are working hard to develop a solution to this problem before the Convention takes effect between our two countries in 2007 or 2008.

In 1982 and 1983, Heino had traveled to start up adoption programs in Central and South America. A slew of both bona fide agencies and crooks followed him. One by one, over the years, most countries revoked their international adoption programs due to internal pressure. There were charges of corruption, kidnapping, and baby selling. Some countries swept out the bad officials and reopened with better ones. Most of these countries ratified the Hague Convention of 1993, and some even made provisions that citizens of countries who have *not* ratified it and set up a central authority cannot adopt from the countries that have. In 1994, Colombia closed, conducted a major investigation, jailed some officials, and then reopened. This country has continued to place children, although in steadily decreasing numbers.

During the Korean War, international adoptions were arranged by highly ethical adoption agencies. Among them was Holt International Children's Services. When war broke out in Vietnam, the agencies extended their services there. But Vietnam did not limit the number of agencies or carefully scrutinize them, as Korea had done. This led to unscrupulous facilitators and scandals. When these problems surfaced, the Vietnamese government decided to form bilateral treaties with various countries in order to protect its children. U.S. adoption agencies with programs in Vietnam had to stop placing children while they waited for the two countries to work out an agreement that both governments could sign. This process took three years, but Vietnam is now moving quickly to license American adoption agencies so that they will be held to the new standards. This is good news indeed, and there are strong indications that Vietnam will once again be efficiently placing children, this time with the new safeguards that protect its children and their adoptive families.

When China opened, Heino wondered which agencies would be permitted to place children. Our agency was among the first. In 1992 we traveled to China and helped coordinate the adoptions of the first two little girls through our agency. China briefly closed its doors early on to eliminate corruption, then later to centralize and control adoptions nationwide under the China Center of Adoption Affairs. As a result, it has the most predictable, well-organized adoption program in the world. Part of the simplicity of the procedure is the result of the legal status of abandoned children, which does not require lengthy court procedures to inform birth parents of their rights. The numbers of Chinese children adopted by nonresidents has risen steadily. Now, however, China has jumped on the domestic-adoption bandwagon. The China Center of Adoption Affairs is keenly interested in setting up foster homes and a domestic adoption program similar to those of the United States and Western Europe.

In 2005 China placed over 7,906 children in the United States. However, at a conference with the director general of the China Center of Adoption Affairs (CCAA), Mr. Lu explained, "The CCAA gets more dossiers [applications from adoptive families] each year. In 2004 CCAA got 1.5 times the total amount of dossiers of 2003. In 2005, it is more than two times of 2003. In 2006, dossiers increased 126 percent but the amount of children in the orphanages is not increasing. In 2003 and 2004, referrals of children decreased 49 percent, in 2005 10 percent and in 2006 16 percent. CCAA hopes the adoption agencies can think about this problem. Abandonment in China is illegal. With our social and economic development, abandonment will be less and less; on the other hand, domestic adoption is getting popular, which is a good tendency."

A Reuters article from December 26, 2005, titled, "China Law Threatens Jail for Sex-Selective Abortions," cites a new law calling for prison terms for doctors and other health workers who assist in revealing the gender of unborn babies, a practice leading to abortions. The new law is expected to give teeth to a government campaign to outlaw the selective abortion of female fetuses and correct an imbalance in the ratio of boys to girls that has grown since China's one-child policy was introduced more than twenty years ago.

"Artificial gender selection can jeopardize China's population structure, leading to social instability," wrote An Jian, a member of China's parliament. China has vowed to reverse the trend of its gender imbalance by 2010. It previously launched a tentative plan to pay moderate pensions to rural parents with no sons, and to educate them that "girls are as good as boys." Traditionally, Chinese couples have preferred to raise male children. As a result, about forty million men may live as frustrated bachelors by 2020.

China ratified the Hague Convention in 2005. Nowhere on earth is the adoption process as predictable as in China. The China Center of Adoption Affairs handles the intake, care, matching, and adoption of children throughout the country in an efficient and orderly manner. China's recognition of the fact that the babies are abandoned simplifies everything, because there are no biological relatives to track down, no signatures to be obtained, no court appearances. However, it is still a requirement that a notice is posted locally indicating that an infant has been found, so that the parents may step forward.

The speed with which China is able to free children for adoption contrasts sharply with the lengthy adoption procedures required for Eastern European and Latin American children who were not abandoned. However, China has become such a popular country among foreign adoptive parents that there is now a long waiting list for a Chinese infant or toddler without special needs. This has resulted in prospective parents in our country being told they will most likely wait at least a year for their child after their dossier is sent to China. In a December 2006 meeting held by the CCAA, new policies and procedures as of May 1st, 2007 were explained to adoption agency representatives. Requirements for prospective couples are more stringent, singles are excluded, and the wait for a child may extend from fifteen months to two years. The projected wait is expected to increase considerably in the future. A bureaucratic bottleneck, such as has developed in China despite the great efficiency of the CCAA in processing adoptions, is one disadvantage of the centralization of adoptions that is now required of Hague Convention countries. As a result, more families may choose in the future to adopt from non-Hague countries to shorten their wait for a child. (Alternatively, they may decide to locate an adoptable child "on their own behalf" in any Hague or non-Hague country that permits this. In such a case, the adoptive parents can work with an agency or facilitator that does not require accreditation or approval, hopefully exercising appropriate caution.)

Both Russia, which has not joined the Convention at this writing, and China are the biggest sources of adopted children for the United States. These countries promote domestic adoptions, but in order to do so effectively, they must launch public-relations campaigns to overcome cultural stigmas and ethnic prejudices. They'll also need to provide monetary incentives and ample housing for prospective adoptive parents. The average resident of many sending countries lives in a tiny, utilitarian apartment, with barely enough space for one child. I've visited our adoption representatives, who live in such apartments.

According to the June 19, 2006, issue of the *Christian Science Monitor*, Russia's President Putin has already put some of these incentives into effect by doubling subsidies for foster families. In recent years, Russia has cracked down on foreign adoptions in response to nationalist lawmakers.

"I believe the situation will begin to improve after Putin's measures, and more people will see the importance of adopting," says Galina Kraniskaya, an adviser to Russia's state *Duma*. A Web site set up by the Ministry of Education, www.usynovite.ru, allows Russian prospective parents to pick the age, sex, eye color, and hair color of their child. The site had 153,267 children on its database the week the article was printed.

By contrast Vietnam welcomes prospective adoptive parents from abroad. The Vietnamese provinces still need foreign funding for social-service projects. Soon after our first trip to China, Heino had traveled to Vietnam and had been coaxed by provincial authorities to build two orphanages. This was a huge expenditure, but the benefits quickly became obvious. Adoptive parents brought home babies and children in excellent physical and emotional health. Their needs were completely fulfilled. The nannies practiced the same communal living style as they did in their villages. Instead of using baby cribs, three nannies per room cared for two or three babies each on bedlike platforms where they slept, ate, and chatted with each other 24-7.

The benefits were substantial…that is, until the government started forming bilateral agreements with various nations and stopped placing children with U.S. citizens until our country signed a similar agreement. Three years later, the United States and Vietnam had finally signed one that was acceptable to both governments. Heino flew back to that country in 2006 to obtain licensure for our agency. By that time, however, Western European agencies were already established in the orphanages we had built.

International adoption programs change with the vagaries of the politics of our country and those of the birth country of the children. There is always talk about the best interest of the child. Unfortunately this is not always reflected in public policy. In 1993 over sixty nations gathered at the Hague, Holland, to conclude the Hague Convention for the Protection of Children and Cooperation in Respect of Intercountry Adoption, but it took the United States another thirteen years to publish the Final Regulations for Accreditation of U.S. Adoption Agencies. The process of applying for accreditation began in October of 2006.

In October of 2000, the United States passed the law required for the treaty to eventually be ratified, the Intercountry Adoption Act (IAA). The U.S. Senate ratified it as required for foreign treaties. President Clinton signed the law. There is a provision in that law that requires the U.S. Department of State to be the Central Authority in the United States.

They say that a revolution can sweep clean, but a reformation points forward and backward at the same time. Anti-adoption forces would love a clean sweep, but better and wiser heads drafted the Hague treaty, the capstone that will reform international adoption. In 2007 the United States is scheduled to ratify the treaty. International adoption should be safer, more predictable, and more stable. Yet no one can control what the sending countries decide. Clamp on a moratorium in order to implement the Convention? Limit the number of American and Western European adoption agencies? Most countries are trying to unite children with birth relatives and are keeping infants available to their nationals for one to four years before making them available to nonresidents. This trend in developing countries, along with their efforts to bolster domestic adoptions and develop an infrastructure for foster care, may well result in declining numbers of adoptions by nonresidents.

Ethiopia is the newest efficient source of adoptable children and has exceeded India in terms of numbers of orphans that have recently been adopted and immigrated to the United States. In 2006, 732 children arrived here, up from 441 the year before. But the general trend downward in several countries shows up in annual statistics for immigration. Look up the U.S. Department of State's "Immigrant Visas Issued to Orphans Coming to U.S." For the first time since 1992, in "World Total for Calendar Years," the sum has decreased instead of increased. In 2005, 22,728 children were brought to the United States. And in 2006, 20,679 children were brought to the United States, in contrast to 22,884 in 2004—decreases that bear watching.

Countries that place children in the United States are also keeping an eye on the statistics. This includes the occasional illegal adoption that comes to light. Unfortunately Americans have been the adoptive parents of the majority of illegally placed children, since the United States has always been the receiving country for more children from abroad than any other nation.

By 1991 numerous sending countries had attempted to regulate intercountry adoption by approaching the U.S. Department of State in the hope of forming bilateral agreements. Heino heard about this development from Dr. William Pierce, who at that time was president of the National Council for Adoption (NCFA) in Washington DC. Pierce had founded this nongovernmental umbrella organization for private adoption agencies. He kept NCFA members informed of pending legislative children's issues and called for action. Pierce explained that the Department of State preferred to negotiate one international treaty, rather than a lot of multilateral agreements. Thus the department had initiated a movement toward a proposed new Hague Convention on intercountry adoption under the auspices of the Hague Conference on Private International Law.

The Hague Conference is an international organization that has been located since 1893 at the International Court of Justice in the Hague, Netherlands. It has given the name "Hague Convention" to many international agreements over more than a century, but the proposed treaty would be the first Hague Convention to deal with intercountry adoption.

Between 1991 and 1993, Heino and many other adoption agency representatives attended study group meetings as consultants to the U.S. Department of State. Thus adoption agencies were invited to give the benefit of long experience to their recommendations on the multilateral treaty, which would be given the formal name of the 1993 Hague Convention on Protection of Children and Cooperation in Respect of Intercountry Adoption. In broad terms, the purpose of the treaty (which is called the Hague Convention on Intercountry Adoption for short) is to strengthen protections for adopted children in the following ways:

- To ensure that intercountry adoptions take place in the best interest of children

- To prevent the abduction, exploitation, sale, or trafficking of children

The treaty was concluded in the Hague, Netherlands, in 1993. Participation in the official celebration of this event had been one of Heino's life goals. He arranged for our four youngest children to join us in Holland for a family reunion. Our son Omar, a soldier in the U.S. Army, was based in Heino's homeland of Germany at the time. We met Omar in Frankfurt and rented a Volkswagen van that would hold two parents and four grown children. The kids nicknamed our van "the turtle." On the Autobahn, Germans driving Mercedes-Benzes and BMWs rocketed past us at a hundred miles per hour. We were all relieved when we crossed the border into Holland, where such a display of speed and power was *verboten*.

The following day, our family's first stop was the Peace Palace, where the International Court of Justice is situated. The architecture of that venerable building was exactly what we had expected. Then the family split off in different directions. Prior to the trip, Rosana and Tatiana had contacted girls they had met the year before at the fiftieth anniversary celebration of the adoption agency in Bogota, Colombia, that had placed them as infants. With great excitement, they boarded a train to meet their Colombian-Dutch friends, while Kirk and Omar visited museums. Heino and I, as members of IVAAN, an international organization, experienced the thrill of watching First Secretary JHA (Hans) van Loon preside over the opening of the Hague Convention. Representatives from sixty-two nations listened intently to the proceedings through earphones. Around the perimeter of the room, simultaneous translators spoke to us all, in various languages, from soundproof booths.

After several years of participation in the Hague study group meetings, Heino was eager to finally hear the standards designed to protect homeless children in Hague-compliant countries. The long process of developing the Hague Convention on Protection of Children and Cooperation in Respect of Intercountry Adoption was concluded on May 29, 1993. Representatives of thirty countries, including the United States, quickly signed the Convention—but this only meant that they would bring the treaty back to their governments for discussions on potential ratification.

At a reception for Hague Convention participants that night in the Mauritshuis Museum, Heino and I were enraptured by the Vermeers, Rembrandts, and Potters on the walls as we listened to energized Hague participants discuss the standards. As I moved through rooms filled with more canvasses of Dutch masters, I exulted in the fact that the Convention had turned a goal of mine into a global requirement. Since 1973 I had written extensive training materials. At first I wrote manuals for an adoptive parent support group, then a series of books that I updated and revised, until the work culminated in *How to Adopt Internationally*, currently in its third printing. I also had written, and was continually revising, a curriculum called "International Adoptive Parenting." Yet fewer than half of our prospective adoptive parents had ever read these materials. As a result, their adoption trips were far more stressful than necessary, and placements of children were fraught with anxiety. At last the Convention put teeth into the requirement that prospective adoptive parents must have a minimum of ten hours of training on international adoptive parenting.

I shared this happy moment with Dr. Pierce before he mingled with the crowd of Hague participants. He had obviously done his homework. Pierce was not only an expert on the Hague Convention, but also well versed in cultural differences. This must have been one of Pierce's shining moments. I watched him move confidently through the international crowd, meeting and greeting. He knew exactly when to bow, when to kiss a hand, and when to place his upright palms together as a sign of respect.

A guiding spirit of the Convention with a fine legal mind, Peter H. Pfund, made the rounds as well. Pfund, who was assistant legal advisor for private international law in the Department of State from 1979 to 1997, had headed up the

U.S. delegation to the Convention for years. He is known for his contributions to the progressive development of private international law, the international legal process, and the United States approach. His article "Prospects for Adoption in the United States" details the progression of steps in the development of the Convention, as well as the efforts to bring the long planning process to a successful conclusion. His article can be found at www.cisg.law.pace.edu/cisg/biblio/pfund1.html.

In the months following our return to the United States, I realized an important difference between a lawyer and a writer: Pfund had been cautious over the timing of U.S. ratification, and I had been too optimistic. The United States wasn't even close to implementation. Heino, who was sixty-eight and a man of action, waited impatiently. He swore he would not retire until the United States had ratified and implemented the Convention, so he could apply for Hague accreditation for Los Niños International Adoption Center. Thirteen years later, on February 15, 2006, the Department of State published the final rules for "accreditation of agencies" under the Intercountry Adoption Act (IAA) of 2000, in the Federal Register, CFR Parts 96, 97, and 98. By that time, Heino was eighty-one, still working, and eagerly looking forward to the implementation of the Hague Convention following the formation of accrediting bodies.

It was now up to the U.S. Department of State to designate qualified public and nonprofit entities to accredit or approve the adoption agencies and individuals seeking to provide adoption services in Convention cases. These accrediting bodies would monitor compliance with Hague standards and would be granted the power to yank accreditation or approval from the wayward.

Heino had absorbed Hague information like a sponge. He has said that the new rules are consistent with the Intercountry Adoption Act of 2000 (IAA) and the Convention. Visit Hague Convention and Intercountry Adoption Act Background http://travel.state.gov/family/adoption/convention/convention_2290.html. The accreditation/approval system does not displace the licensing standards of each American state. Instead the rules create new federal requirements for adoption agencies and individuals handling adoption cases.

After waiting for so many years, Heino was totally disgusted when he heard from official sources that the Convention is expected to enter into force for the United States sometime in 2007, but quite possibly this will happen as late as the middle of 2008. By that time, private adoption agencies must have received accreditation in order to provide adoption services involving the United States and another Convention country, or they must be working under the supervision of an accredited agency in each case. Attorneys and for-profit organizations that are arranging adoptions from Convention countries will generally need to be "approved" (as opposed to "accredited"), so they will be held to high standards as well.

One benefit of the new rules is that prospective adoptive parents will finally have some guidance as to ethical and financial standards. This will take a lot of the guesswork out of selecting an adoption agency or attorney. The Department of State will publish, and update quarterly, a list of accredited adoption agencies and approved persons.

Keep the following differentiations in mind when you're selecting either an agency or another type of adoptive service provider:

- Accreditation—Nonprofit private adoption agencies that arrange one hundred or more placements a year must apply for full accreditation that will last for three to five years. Agencies that arrange fewer adoptions may apply for either full accreditation or temporary accreditation.

- Temporary Accreditation—As noted above, only nonprofit private adoption agencies that placed fewer than one hundred children in the calendar year 2005 are eligible to apply for temporary accreditation if they so choose, rather than full accreditation. This status will last one year for agencies that placed less than one hundred children in 2005 and two years for agencies that placed less than fifty, but it must be followed by full accreditation before the temporary accreditation expires. Temporary accreditation is only available to agencies that have practiced international adoption for three years.

- Approval—For-profit entities or persons placing children (such as attorneys) are generally expected to apply for an approval status that will last three to five years, if they are responsible for arranging adoptions for other people. Like private nonprofit agencies, these for-profit service providers may also work as supervised providers rather than apply for approval status of their own.

It is important to note that parents adopting abroad on their own behalf are completely exempt from any accreditation/approval requirement. This is a very significant exception to the rule. It may encourage many more families to arrange for themselves what used to be a common practice of parent-initiated or parent-identified adoptions. In countries that permit individual families to adopt on their own, parents may decide to take this route in an effort to avoid the bottleneck of waiting families that may result when adoptions are centralized in countries where not many orphans are being processed for adoption by the central government. Those of us who adopted our children in the 1970s from Latin American countries often had no choice but to arrange our own adoptions, since few U.S. agencies had intercountry adoption programs at that time. This was how Heino and I adopted our Colombian-born children, Rosana and Tatiana in 1973, and Omar in 1983. Their adoptions were the catalyst for my research, my writing, and my guidance of adoptive parents.

Michael and Deborah McCurdy adopted baby Mark in Colombia two years after we adopted the twins. "Parent-initiated adoptions were challenging," says Deborah, "but the benefit for the children was that many more found homes in this way than would otherwise have been the case."

It is also important to remember that private nonprofit agencies that do not place children may choose to act solely as supervised providers under the responsibility of an accredited agency, instead of seeking any accreditation of their own. This may be the logical choice for small agencies that provide only home studies and post-adoption services and cannot easily afford the considerable costs associated with accreditation. The fact that a local agency is not accredited does not suggest in any way that its home study services and post-placement services do not meet high standards. (Prospective parents can check out the reputation of any agency through the state office that licensed it, or through adoptive parents who have used that agency in the past.) Agencies that only perform home studies are exempt from accreditation. A primary provider must approve the study.

In the case of any agency working as a supervised provider, the accredited agency that is actually identifying and placing the child is responsible for making sure that all needed adoption services will be provided by one agency or the other. In many cases, it is not practical for the accredited agency that is placing the child to provide the home study for a geographically distant adoptive family, so agencies in different states already typically work as a team in this way.

The Convention clarifies the six adoption services that prospective adoptive parents can expect from an agency that qualifies for temporary or full accreditation, or by its supervised provider in some cases. The placing agency must spell out the details of these services in its contract. This requirement whisks away another curtain of mystery regarding adoption agencies. The Department of State lists these services as follows:

1.   Identifying a child for adoption and arranging the adoption

2.   Securing consent to termination of parental rights and to adoption

3. Performing a home study and report on prospective adoptive parent(s) or a background study or report on a child

4. Making a nonjudicial determination of a child's best interests and of the appropriateness of an adoptive placement

5. Monitoring a case after a child has been placed with prospective adoptive parent(s) until final adoption

6. Assuming custody of a child and providing childcare or any other social service because of a pending disruption of the placement

The Hague differentiates between post-adoption cases and post-placement cases. The term post- adoption applies in the following example: When Baby Emma is adopted abroad, new documents are issued, including

- a final decree that states the names of her new parents;

- a passport that confirms her national origins and her new name.

The IAA deems this a final, completed adoption. And when little Emma is granted an IR-3 visa by the U.S. Consulate abroad it triggers an automatic U.S. Certificate of Citizenship—provided that both parents traveled to adopt her.

Although agencies prefer that both spouses travel for the adoption, some countries, including China and Guatemala, require only one parent to travel. These are also considered post-adoption cases by the IAA. However, U.S. CIS requires readoption in the child's new state of residence if an IR-4 visa is issued. Fortunately, some states recognize a foreign final adoption decree, which eliminates the need for a full adoption in the child's new state of residence.

Although not required by the Hague, the child's country of origin may require post-adoption reports over a specific length of time.

The Hague judges cases as post-placement in the following example: Baby Caleb leaves his homeland under a guardianship or another type of incomplete adoption. The U.S. Consulate abroad issues an IR-4 visa. Post-placement reports are required until little Caleb is adopted in his new state of residence, and possibly beyond, by his country of origin.

Only accredited or supervised providers may conduct post-placement supervision and generate the reports. Caleb will remain an alien in the United States until his adoptive parents apply for and receive his U.S. Certificate of Citizenship.

- **Tip:** Adoptive parents who refuse to comply and agencies that fail to provide the reports may cause serious problems for themselves.

The Hague does not regulate visas or citizenship. Unfortunately, in post-placement cases such as Caleb's, some parents don't follow through—due to ignorance or procrastination. Caleb could fall through the cracks and not know he's an alien until years later, when he needs proof of citizenship. This problem must be addressed by Congress.

Hopefully the Convention's safeguards that protect children will influence other nations to join the Convention. From October 2004 to September 2005 (FY 2005), U.S. citizens adopted 13,241 children from countries that joined the Convention. In FY 2006, they adopted 11,838. This accounts for over half of all intercountry adoptions in both years.

*Top 10 Convention Countries from which U.S.
Citizens Adopted in FY 2005 and 2006:*

Country	Number of adoptions		2006
1. China	7,906	1. China	6,493
2. Guatemala	3,783	2. Guatemala	4,135
3. India	322	3. Colombia	344
4. Colombia	291	4. India	320
5. Philippines	271	5. Philippines	245
6. Mexico	88	6. Mexico	70
7. Poland	73	7. Poland	67
8. Thailand	72	8. Brazil	66
9. Brazil	66	9. Thailand	56
10. Moldova	54	10. Japan	42

Note: China became a Convention country in January of 2006.

*Top 10 Non-Convention Countries
from which U.S. citizens Adopted in FY 2005 and 2006:*

Country	Number of Adoptions		2006
1. Russia	4,639	1. Russia	3,706
2. S. Korea	1,630	2. S. Korea	1,376
3. Ukraine	821	3. Ethiopia	732
4. Kazakhstan	755	4. Kazakhstan	587
5. Ethiopia	441	5. Ukraine	460
6. Haiti	234	6. Liberia	353
7. Liberia	183	7. Haiti	309
8. Taiwan	141	8. Taiwan	187
9. Nigeria	65	9. Vietnam	163
10. Jamaica	63	10. Nepal	66

For more information on implementation of the Convention, the Department of State suggests checking travel.state.gov or e-mailing AdoptionUSCA@state.gov.

The handwriting is on the wall. An article titled *After Years of Rapid Growth, Foreign Adoptions Drop Sharply*, in *The Houston Chronicle*, January 7th, 2007, reiterates this forecast. *Declines were recorded last year in nearly all countries that recently have been the top sources of adopted children—China, Russia, South Korea and Ukraine among them. Increases from less familiar alternatives—Ethiopia, Liberia, Haiti and Vietnam—partly offset the drop, but some experts think the era of constantly surging foreign adoption has ended. "The huge growth rates you saw in the 90's—I think that's over," said Thomas DiFilipo, president of the Joint Council on International Children's Services.* I expect that fewer children will be adopted internationally by the end of the next decade, 2016. Yet thanks to the Hague Convention, their adoptive families should enjoy a predictable and trustworthy process. During this decade, the number of adoption agencies will probably decrease due to the inability of some to meet the high standards for agencies set by the Hague Convention. It may be that agencies that make the grade will compete for dwindling sources of children available abroad. On a more optimistic note, some people feel that new countries will open up because of Hague safeguards, despite an initial decline in numbers.

- **Tip:** If you're thinking of adopting abroad, start the process as soon as possible.

When the Hague Convention goes into effect, it will not impact your own adoption as long as you have already filed Form I-600A. Filing this simple form with the Citizenship and Immigration Services (CIS) is the first step in the process of getting immigration clearance for your child. It is generally done at the time you begin your home study—or, in some states, just after home study completion. Provided that you file at the earliest possible time, you should not have to worry about the possibility of any changes in federal immigration procedures complicating your adoption, or delaying the child's arrival, when you are part way through the process. Section 505(b) of the IAA confirms that these adoption cases are protected during the transition. Visit http://travel.state.gov/pdf/ Prospective_Adoptive_Parents_Guide.pdf.

The international adoption agency that you are currently considering, and the specific country from which you hope to adopt, may not be a viable choice in a few years. A lot of adoption agencies are already in transition, giving thought to forming mergers and partnerships to pool their resources for Hague accreditation expenses and/or for the costs of maintaining adoption programs abroad.

As an alternative, if you decide not to adopt internationally, consider adopting an American-born child, particularly an older "waiting child" in foster care, or perhaps an infant or toddler of another race. Bone up on adoption through your state's child protective services department or, if you would like a baby, gather information from local private agencies. Thousands of children of all races are in public and private foster homes, and many of them are available for adoption. Bear in mind that most of the available American "children who wait" are of school age and/or have significant medical, emotional, or developmental challenges—which is why the international adoption of very young children became so popular in the first place. (This very popularity, however, has had the great benefit of making intercountry adoption, as well as transracial adoption, highly visible and well accepted in many communities across the country.)

As Howard Alstein, professor in the School of Social Work at the University of Maryland, wrote in the *Baltimore Sun*, "Why reject what we know: Children of one race raised in families of another race develop into productive, emotionally healthy, assured, racially comfortable adults."

It may take longer for prospective adoptive parents to find a suitable agency, or for the processing of adoptions, but many children overseas will continue to need loving homes in greater numbers than developing countries can provide.

INDEX

978-0-595-40206-9
0-595-40206-2